I'VE ALWAYS LOOKED UP TO GIRAFFES

I'VE ALWAYS LOOKED UP TO GIRAFFES

Discover why and how some people and organizations
stand head and shoulders above the crowd
and inspire others to reach new heights.

FOREWORD BY KEVIN FREIBERG

HUGH GOULDTHORPE & BILL GRAVITT

To Mary Frances, Nelle,
Anne-Merle, Carol and Karen

Published in the USA

ISBN 0-9718519-0-5

How to Read and Learn from "Giraffes"

I*'ve Always Looked Up To Giraffes* is not your typical book. There are no chapters *per se,* but a series of thoughts, ideas and principles designed to stimulate and challenge your thinking. Turn to any page in the book and you will find a simple, declarative thought that can help you in your business or personal life.

Of course, we want you to read the book from cover to cover to discover the many tidbits of wisdom presented in a simple, understandable format. Once you've done this, we believe you will read it again and again and put into practice these tried and true principles.

As the saying goes, "READ it…you'll like it!"

CONTENTS

"If you pick up a starving dog and make him prosperous, he will not bite you. That is the principle difference between dog and man."

— Mark Twain

FOREWORD
by Kevin Freiberg

We are living in a time of unprecedented change and great peril. Employees faced with many distractions need hope, focus, and a sense of direction. Customers who are more educated, sophisticated, demanding, and less tolerant want to do business only with companies who will keep their promises. Nervous investors are looking for leaders with a clear vision, who understand the market, and have the ability to inspire the best in their people. Everywhere you turn you can hear the call for leaders—people who aren't afraid to step into the breach, instill confidence, and deliver the goods. This book seeks to answer that call. It reads like a daily devotional for people who want to put on the mantle of leadership and make a mark in the world.

With this book Hugh Gouldthorpe is sure to make his mark. Curiosity inevitably gets the best of Hugh and many of us are better off for it. These pages are a wonderful tribute to the spirit of lifelong learning that possesses this indefatigable sixty-two-year-old. "Goldie," as his friends and colleagues affectionately call him, is one of those people who brings sheer energy into a room. Anyone who has spent even a few brief moments with this character—and he is a character—cannot help but be captivated by his zest for life and his contagious enthusiasm. The good news for you and me is that this same passion burns through the pages of this book. Hugh Gouldthorpe has channeled this energy into becoming a connoisseur of extraordinary leaders and great companies. Now he shares his wisdom with us.

It would be very difficult to walk away from a conversation with "Goldie" and not be aware that you have been in the presence of a true gentleman. He's a fierce competitor with extremely high standards. He doesn't tolerate mediocrity in himself or others. But in the end Hugh Gouldthorpe has a knack for drawing the best out of people by helping them develop confidence in themselves. What you will read in the pages that follow is what "Goldie" lives. He embodies the values and attributes we look for in every leader.

As Head Cheerleader, Hugh is one of the catalytic agents behind the incredible success story at Owens&Minor, the nation's largest distributor of name-brand medical/surgical supplies. Owens&Minor has received numerous awards including being named by *Information Week Magazine* as the number one most innovative user of information technology in the nation. Obviously, this doesn't happen without turned-on, passionate leaders at all levels who contribute to a culture of commitment. In this book you will find many of the strategies and tools that Hugh and his teammates have used to rally the people and shape the culture at Owens&Minor.

I've Always Looked Up To Giraffes is loaded with stories and anecdotes that are a mirror image of this master storyteller himself. They are anchored in timeless principles and common sense. Practical, witty, and insightful, this book reflects the playfulness and wisdom of a seasoned executive who hasn't lost his sense of humor. It is a light-hearted read chock-full of profound insights. Are you operating in a time-constrained world where you're going ninety miles per hour with your hair on fire? Are you trying to do more with less? Then you will find the quick, bite-size chapters and fun illustrations refreshing.

As you read on, you will find an agile, thoughtful, and engaging mind bent on persuading us to reflect upon why some leaders and some organizations tower above the rest. Drawing upon the successful practices at Wal*Mart, Ritz-Carlton Hotels, Southwest Airlines, Ukrop's Super Markets, and others, Gouldthorpe shows us what separates the best from the rest. This easy-to-read collection of what-to-dos, how-tos, and what-not-to-dos is a sincere and valuable reflection of what Hugh has learned about success and failure throughout his career.

This book is written for those of you who want to make a difference in your organizations—regardless of title and position. It's for those who want to revitalize work, rekindle commitment, and reestablish customer loyalty. It's for those who want to go home at the end of the day emotionally charged instead of emotionally drained. Take one principle a week for a year, reflect upon it, internalize it, and then put into practice. I predict you will become a stronger leader and a better person. You will also experience more freedom and more fulfillment at work. Easier said than done you say? Hugh Gouldthorpe would be the first to admit that the journey he urges you to embark upon is not for the faint at heart. Following the sage advice in *I've Always Looked Up To Giraffes* will not guarantee success. But while the world in which we live cries out for GUTSY leaders, what's the alternative to trying?

Kevin Freiberg
San Diego, California
November 2001

PREFACE

What's up with a business book about giraffes? What do great leaders and giraffes have in common? What are the similarities? The answer to these questions is simple: A lot!

In her book, *Tall Blondes,* Lynn Sherr describes fascinating characteristics and facts about giraffes. I have used her insight and wisdom to make the comparisons between leaders and giraffes.

Think about it. Giraffes stand head and shoulders above the crowd. We all have to look up to them. The best leaders stand head and shoulders above the crowd and are admired by those they lead.

Giraffes, like great leaders, are able to reach things that others can't begin to fathom. They do this in a very competent manner without calling attention to themselves.

Giraffes have wonderful vision; in fact, a giraffe can spot a person a mile away. Likewise, great leaders have vision that helps them lead their organizations to new heights. Look at a giraffe's eye and you'll find it to be soft and compassionate. The same holds true for great leaders. Both communicate with their eyes.

In Africa, the giraffe is considered to be the symbol of friendship. Talk with great leaders and you'll find them to be kind, caring, friendly and most approachable. Great leaders and giraffes have lots of friends.

There are at least nine different patterns of giraffes, and yet giraffes make no such distinction among their peers. These are the most politically correct members of the animal kingdom. As they do not discriminate based on the color of other giraffes' skin, the same can be said of great leaders, as the color of one's skin plays no role in their evaluation of others.

Giraffes are able to go long distances in short periods of time. In fact, a giraffe can run in the neighborhood of 35-40 miles per hour and do so in a most graceful manner. Great leaders, in order to accomplish their goals and objectives, move rapidly and confidently in a manner that doesn't create chaos in others.

Giraffes are tireless animals, as they sleep only about a half hour a day. Tireless is a word sometimes used to describe great leaders and their quest to get the job done.

Giraffes are born with horns that they don't shed. Horns in animals are linked to antenna which in turn is linked to perception and reception. Great leaders are very receptive to input which in turn creates perceptions that help them make decisions.

Giraffes are very competitive animals that can kick in four directions. Their 12-inch-wide hooves, along with the leverage created by their long legs, deliver a powerful blow. Competitive is a word we associate with great leaders who do not know the meaning of the word "can't." They are committed to "blowing away" their competition and taking the top spot.

Most of all, giraffes have a very different look. Great leaders understand that to be successful in today's world one must have a different look and be willing to try new and different things. To them, average is where the best of the worst meets the worst of the best, and they know that people and companies that settle for average will never stand head and shoulders above the crowd.

We hope you will enjoy reading *I've Always Looked Up To Giraffes* as much as we have enjoyed writing and illustrating it.

Hugh Gouldthorpe and Bill Gravitt

IT'S GOING TO RAIN BECAUSE THE COWS ARE LYING DOWN
Great Leaders are Great Storytellers

As a young boy growing up in Warrenton, Virginia (population 2,500), I was exposed to many stories. These stories focused on the weather, crops, animals, and local characters. These stories were interesting, educational, fascinating, and, most of all, memorable.

One of the great stories I vividly remember relates to the fact that you can predict it's going to rain if the cows are lying down in the field. If they are standing, you can expect nice weather.

I can remember times when the cows were lying down and the weather was beautiful. Obviously this was contradictory to the legend and in my mind disproved it. When I approached my Dad and told him this, his answer always was, "Well, Son, some of these cows are just tired."

Whether the story is true or not, to this day when I see cows lying down in the field I feel it's going to rain. There is a lesson for all of us in this, in that stories are powerful, and we remember them. We might not remember a bunch of facts or details, but we'll remember an interesting and fascinating story.

Tell Your Story

Think of the speakers who hold your attention. They are interesting, dynamic, and great storytellers. They use actual life experiences to get their points across.

One of the greatest storytellers I ever had the privilege to hear is H. Ross Perot. Ross is a great businessman, Chairman of Perot Systems, and the author of *Ross Perot, My Life and the Principles for Success*. Ross mesmerizes his audiences by telling stories about people he's met on planes, overseas, in the subway, in schools, or on the street. He then shares the questions they asked and how he responded. He is so good at storytelling that he makes you feel like you were part of the experience and that you were present during the conversation. In fact, once he starts a story, you never want it to end.

A "Wall" of Stories

Another great storyteller was Sam Walton of Wal*Mart fame. "Mr. Sam" was a master at telling stories, and the stories that have evolved about Mr. Sam and Wal*Mart are legendary. When Mr. Sam died the stories were passed on to others in the organization and are part of the spirit, aura, and culture of the vast, fast-growing Wal*Mart empire.

When Leon Leonwood Bean, founder of L.L. Bean, introduced his famous Maine hunting shoes, he guaranteed them not to leak.

These shoes, which were so much lighter than the heavy leather woodman's boots of his day, were unique in that they had rubber soles. Unfortunately, of the first 100 pairs he sold to fellow sportsmen, 90 pairs were returned when the stitching gave way. However, true to his word, he refunded all his customers' money. That story has been told and retold to Bean employees and customers and it's a part of their legend and culture. And because of that, L.L. Bean is known for its unbelievable customer service and for providing 100% satisfaction on every product they sell.

One of the great storytellers of all time is Herb Kelleher, the recently retired CEO of Southwest Airlines. He is a legend in the airline business and his storytelling has perpetuated the Southwest culture. In their best-selling book, *NUTS!,* Jackie and Kevin Freiberg quote Boeing's president and CEO, Phil Condit, who states, "Herb is the ultimate storyteller and his stories get repeated and retold which form the fabric of the Southwest culture." The Freibergs go on to point out, however, that Herb is not the only storyteller at Southwest, in that he has created a culture of highly spirited people to carry their stories forward.

Company Stories

Tell stories of your company and its successes to everyone. You want to make sure that your employees and customers know that they are part of a legacy. Relate stories about your customers, about how you were able to get the business and about what that meant to the company. Share stories about your teammates and about heroic efforts. These stories become part of your history, culture, and values. They remind people of who they are, what they are all about, and what contributes to their success.

At Owens&Minor, we are so proud to tell our teammates the stories that have propelled us to the top of the medical/surgical distribution industry. When we share these stories with them, they feel a sense of pride and a feeling that they are working for a company that has a great tradition of taking care of its teammates, customers, suppliers, and shareholders.

At Owens&Minor we share as many stories as we can with our teammates. When a teammate takes it on their own to make a delivery after hours or works late in the office correcting a customer service problem, we not only tell the story but reward them as well. When you reward people who go the extra mile and share their stories with others, it infects your entire organization. It's a great feeling to work with people who take pride in everything they do and who always strive to go the extra mile. Storytelling fuels the emotions of others and acts as a catalyst to enhance your organization's effectiveness.

No End to the Story

Make sure the stories about your organization "fall like rain." If you do, no one will ever accuse you of lying down when it comes to being successful in business.

 Giraffism: Stories are fascinating, fun, interesting— but most of all—memorable. They perpetuate and solidify a company's culture.

RUDENESS IS A CONTROLLABLE EMOTION

If you're like me, I can put up with a lot of things in this world, but the one thing that is intolerable to me is rudeness. I can understand people making mistakes and poor judgment, but there is absolutely NO excuse for being rude to others or putting them down.

Think about the rude people you know. They all fit a profile. They are usually loud, expert on everything, sarcastic, cute, and very poor listeners. Their goal is to dominate every conversation because that allows them to always be in control. They think they are "cool." They are cool all right, so cool that no one wants to be around them. On the other hand, we have those warm individuals who smile and make us feel wanted and good. They like and respect those with whom they come in contact and they let them know that they care and are interested in them.

Be a Positive Force

Recently I was flying on a major airline. The flight attendant serving us (and I use that term loosely) was one of the rudest people I have ever met. The people sitting around me were so nice and simply expecting to be treated like customers. The flight attendant, besides chewing and popping her gum, literally threw the bags of trail mix to everyone. Her answers to questions were "Yeah," and "Nope." After a while, I stopped her and said, "I bet you hated coming to work this morning!" "Yeah," she replied, to which I responded, "It shows!"

She reminded me of a policy at Disney World that states, "If you work here, you're on stage." What a great policy, and one that should be the *modus operandi* of every company and certainly this airline.

Talk and Walk

One of the things that you can do is to lead others by example. The way you treat your workers and your kids is the way they treat other people. Show people by your own actions the way things should be done. Be a role model and lead the way.

Over the years I have witnessed the firing of many leaders. They understood the business and the importance of helping people succeed. They demanded discipline but unfortunately had none themselves. Most of all they refused to live up to the standards set for others. They had the opportunity to be a real role model but they allowed their egos and their "I'm bigger than life" attitude to do them in. What a shame and waste of human talent. Once one thinks and acts like they are the greatest, they are in for a real downfall.

Energize Others

There is no doubt that we all like to be around people who are positive, who get things done, and who delight in helping others. One of the ways that you can help others is to let them know that you're interested and that you want them to succeed. When people know that you're on their side, they will try harder and give it their all. They will always try to exceed your expectations. When one is curt, rude and indifferent to others, people's attitudes are "I could care less!"

Reason and Emotion

People are persuaded by reason but moved by emotion. That's why the positive and upbeat manner in which you present things is key. The words, tone of voice and mannerisms you use will determine how effective your team or organization will be. If you are rude, it will transfer to others and perpetuate an intolerable habit. Winston Churchill summed it up best when he told a lady that her dog was kind of ugly. She responded, "Sir, you are rude." Sir Winston rapidly replied, "Yes ma'am, but I can correct mine." Rudeness is a controllable emotion…control it yourself and help others do the same.

 Giraffism: Rude people have a negative effect on those they touch and leave others feeling deflated.

SIT IT OUT OR DANCE? DANCE!

I'm one of those people who loves all kinds of music. It can be Van Morrison, Elton John, a Sousa march, Andrew Lloyd Weber's brilliant musical scores, Garth Brooks, a Mozart symphony, or Etta James wailing the blues. There's some real depth, positive messages and words of wisdom in many songs…words that can impact our lives.

One of the best albums to hit the charts in the last few years is by Lee Ann Womack entitled, *I Hope You Dance.* It also happens to be the best song on the album and was the country music song of the year.

It's a beautiful song with some wonderful philosophy about life.

The first two lines of the song state,

> *"I hope you never lose your sense of wonder*
> *You get your fill to eat but always keep that hunger"*

The most successful people I know are those who are always seeking the new. They are curious about everything and feel that every day is a learning experience for them. They are never too old to learn and they garner as much feedback as humanly possible.

Lines five through eight go like this:

"I hope you still feel small when you stand beside the ocean
Whenever one door closes
I hope one more opens
Promise me that you'll give faith the fighting chance"

Great leaders and people are never too big or important to meet with and talk with others. They treat everyone the same, whether they are the president of a large corporation or someone who works as a clerk in the mailroom. They love and respect others regardless of the others' status in life.

Great leaders are also realistic. They know that not everything works out as planned and that they will fail many times before they succeed. However, they believe in themselves and the people around them and know that they can overcome any obstacle placed before them. To them, success comes in cans…I can, we can and you can!

The second part of the song goes like this:

"I hope you never fear those mountains in the distance
Never settle for the path of least resistance
Living might mean taking chances but they're worth taking
Loving might be a mistake but it's worth making
Don't let some hell-bent heart leave you bitter
When you come close to selling out reconsider

Give the heavens above more than just a passing glance
and when you get the choice to sit it out or dance
I hope you dance"

Dare to be different. Don't be afraid to take chances or make mistakes. The only people who don't make mistakes are the people who don't do anything. And when you do make a mistake, admit it! The six most important words in the English language are "I admit that I was wrong!"

Three Kinds of People

There are three kinds of people in this world...those who make things happen, those who watch things happen, and those who wonder what happened!

If you sit it out, you either watch things happen or wonder what's happening. But if you dance you're active, involved and moving.

So, make it a practice to dance your way through life. Be creative, try new steps, and "navigate" around the "floor." Don't be shy, and use all of your God-given talents to be the best you can be.

Be one of those people who love to make things happen...and DANCE! DANCE! DANCE!

 Giraffism: The world will pass you by if you're not passionate about life.

SUCCESS COMES IN CANS
I Can…You Can…We Can

The most successful people I've met in my life are those who believe that one's attitude will determine one's altitude. People who believe in themselves are self-starters, proactive, and very much into caring about and developing others.

They know that successful people and successful organizations believe they can handle any job given to them. These organizations and people have vision, energy, and a desire to be the best at what they do. They practice the philosophy that "we're determined to make a difference." One of the most successful organizations I know of is Scott & Stringfellow, one of the South's oldest and most prestigious brokerage firms. Chairman Buford Scott and President and CEO John Sherman have set standards that have perpetuated the firm's image and proficiency. Great Scott…they are good.

I Can

Great leaders are very adept at turning negatives into positives. They are the Norman Vincent Peales of their organization. They know there is a light at the end of a tunnel and it's not a train coming the other way. To them, the glass is always half full. They operate with integrity and have a passion for what they do. It's hard to defeat passion, as it drives us to accomplish a goal or make a difference. Losing or being defeated never enters the great leaders' minds as they are always in it to win it. They don't look at anything they have done in the past as a failure. They understand that we all make mistakes and that learning from mistakes is part of the building process. Always, however, in the forefront of their minds is the phrase, "I can do it." Those are the four words that guide them through the tough and difficult times.

You Can

Great leaders transfer their feelings to others. They are truly infectious and touch the lives of those they lead in a most positive way. They provide guidance and direction and have a sincere desire for their teammates to succeed. One of the questions they consistently pose to teammates is, "What can I do to help you succeed?" Great leaders like their people too much to let them fail. They understand that their success depends on the success of the people they lead. Stewart Roberson, Superintendent of Schools for Hanover County, Virginia, epitomizes these principles. And because of his leadership, Hanover County Schools are among the best in the state.

Great leaders are always supporting and cheering their teammates along. They listen to them and share their thoughts and wisdom. Great leaders don't assume anything and they make sure that everyone is in the loop and knows what's taking place.

We Can

There is no doubt that teamwork is the key to success. No one individual can do it alone. Everyone brings something to the table. Some people are more talented and bring more than others, but each individual contribution is key. It's like putting together a basketball team. If you have five centers, you'll most likely get all of the rebounds, however you'll have trouble getting the ball down the court. Likewise, if you have five guards you'll get the ball down the court, but once you shoot and miss you probably won't get it back. Great leaders are able to blend the talents of their teammates in order that everyone makes a contribution. They encourage their teammates to take the initiative and utilize their skills and talents within a team environment. And when they do this, the team they put together is second to none.

Success truly comes in cans, and great leaders—like the great artists they are—paint a picture where beauty is truly in the eyes of the beholder.

 Giraffism: If you think you can, you can.

TREADING H₂0 JUST KEEPS YOU AFLOAT (BARELY)

The hot, humid Richmond, Virginia summers conjure up many images in people's minds. One of those images involves the ocean, the "rivah" (Richmonders' word for "river"), a swimming pool, or a favorite swimming hole.

I was at our neighborhood pool and I watched those in the deep end. A few were diving off the board and swimming quickly to the sides to dive in again. Some were swimming laps at a rapid pace. The majority, however, were treading water, enjoying the coolness of the pool.

As I watched those treading water, it was obvious that they were comfortable and the cool water lured them into a very relaxed state. I also noted, however, that they were going nowhere and that they were getting tired just trying to stay afloat.

The same holds true for people and organizations that get lured into thinking that they know it all and that they are the best. They become satisfied with the norm. And when they do this, they are in trouble. Their thoughts become shallow and they fail to see the necessity for change. They simply continue with business as usual and they don't recognize that the tide is changing. Once the tide changes, they have to revert to a reactive mode and that takes so much more energy than being proactive. It places stress on the organization and its people, and it's a tiring experience.

Get Your Feet Wet

Great companies and individuals are eager to try out new things. Sometimes their efforts fail, but they modify what they are doing to make it successful.

If you want to compete successfully in today's marketplace, you need to test the waters. Look at what is working for you and what isn't. Determine if your policies and procedures are in the best interests of your company, but more importantly—your customers.

Find out your customers' likes and dislikes, and determine what they are looking for from you in terms of service. Talk with and not to them and find out what you need to do to exceed their expectations. Too many companies and people make the mistake of trying to guess what their customers want. Great customer service organizations practice what I call the ASK (Always Seek Knowledge) theory. This allows them to be proactive in their communication and easily meet the customers' needs.

"Swim" the Extra Mile

Olympic swimmers understand that with the proper training and conditioning they have a chance to walk away with the gold. They also know that it takes hard work and dedication to reach the top of their profession but that when they do, there's no greater feeling than being a winner. They tread water after the race is won and celebrate their victory. This allows them to catch their wind for the next event.

The same holds true for great leaders and organizations. They know there is no greater feeling than being a winner and they go the extra mile to ensure they experience this feeling. They surround themselves with people who want to excel and be the best at what they do.

In a conversation with Ross Perot, I asked him what kind of people he looked for to hire for his organization. He quickly replied, "People who want to win." I then asked him what he did when he ran out of applicants with this attitude. Without batting an eye, he replied, "I hire people who don't want to lose." What a great philosophy, and one that can have a great impact on us and our organizations.

Take the Plunge

So if you want to be the best, you need to take the plunge and dive in, head first. Don't be timid and don't waste your time treading water. Don't be afraid to try new and different things. Don't drown in old thoughts. Be creative; try new "strokes" and take the lead. If you do, you'll think of treading water as water over the dam.

 Giraffism: If you don't take risks and chances, you'll never win the race.

IT'S OK TO BE "PIGGY"

Lexington is located in central North Carolina, between Greensboro and Charlotte. It's a wonderful community of 20,000 people where furniture and barbecue are king. It's also the home of Lexington Barbecue.

Have you ever had any southern barbecue? It makes no difference how you answer this question, because the answer is a flat out NO unless you've eaten at Lexington Barbecue.

They are open six days a week and serve an average 1,000 customers per day. What makes them so special and so successful?

To answer this question one has to look no further than the Monk family, the owners of the business. Mr. Monk senior started the business in 1962, and his reputation for providing great, tasty barbecue and wonderful service is unparalleled in the industry. Mr. Monk, his wife and children have all been active in the business and today son, Rick, oversees the day-to-day operation.

Be There

On my first visit to Lexington Barbecue to meet Rick I found him outside the rear of the restaurant hosing out the trash and garbage receptacles. I asked him why he was doing that and he replied,

"I wouldn't ask any of my employees to do something I wouldn't." That was my first tip as to why this business has been successful.

The second sign as to why they are successful was the fact that Rick took time to talk with me and gave me his full attention. I was there at lunch time, and a big percentage of the 1,000 customers who dine there every day was coming through the doors. He excused himself for a moment, but came back and gave me his undivided attention. He truly understands and practices the principle that great leaders are always busy, but never in a hurry.

Be Knowledgeable

After spending time with Rick I ordered lunch and was treated to royal service. The waitress I had was knowledgeable and polite and helped me understand the difference between the different barbecue trays they offered. She pointed out to me that Lexington Barbecue only uses pork shoulders that are cooked about nine hours over hickory and oak coals. She informed me that they salted the meat before cooking but did no basting. And she proudly stated that this is the Lexington-style barbecue. She understood the importance of keeping the customer informed and letting them know what separates Lexington Barbecue from its competitors.

Treat Employees Like Royalty

After eating I talked with other employees, many of whom had been there 15 years and longer, as to why they like working at Lexington Barbecue. They all mentioned that the Monk family treated them like family and that they cared about them. They mentioned specific instances when they needed time off to take care of their family or some unforeseen circumstance. They pointed out that this was never an issue, as the Monk family believes that one's family always comes first. They also mentioned that Lexington Barbecue is closed on Sundays to allow its employees to rest and/or attend the religious service of their choice.

As I reflect on my day at Lexington Barbecue, it is obvious that Rick Monk understands the simple principle that if he takes care of his employees and customers and exercises sound business principles he will continue to be successful and grow. And when you combine these principles with their wonderful smoked products, their sales and reputation will continue to go up and up.

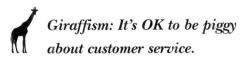 *Giraffism: It's OK to be piggy about customer service.*

Follow the Yellow Brick Road

Not long ago my family and I attended a show entitled, *The Wizard of Oz on Ice*. I'm sure that most of you are familiar with this magnificent story. It's a wonderful tale packed with an interesting array of diverse characters. Some of the characters are strong and some are very weak.

If you think about it, these characters are like people with whom we interact every day. We all know some Wicked Witch of the West who delights in tantalizing and making life miserable for others. Likewise, we know some people like Glinda, the Good Witch of the North, whose main goal in life is to help others. We also know a lot of cowardly lions without courage, tin men without hearts, and some scarecrows who don't think as well as others. We all know some wizards who pretend to be tough and yet are kind and gentle when you really get to know them. And last but not least, we know some Dorothys who are strong, determined, and who have a heart of gold.

Know the Players

The most successful people I know on this earth are those who care for and have an interest in others. In *The Wizard of Oz*, Dorothy takes an interest in everyone she meets and has real compassion for them. She understands their shortcomings but doesn't let it affect her feelings for them. She genuinely wants to help them succeed and attain their life's goals. She's what I call a giraffe leader—one who truly stands head and shoulders above the crowd.

Don't Be a Doomsayer

One of the things Dorothy understood was that she had to be strong for her friends. She realized that they were struggling and she knew that she had to buoy their thoughts. When they got discouraged she was there for them, always offering words of encouragement and telling them they could do it. Like the great leader she was, she understood the importance of a positive attitude.

Have a Clear Vision

Dorothy had this clear vision of where she wanted to go and what she needed to accomplish. She had a goal of getting back to Kansas and to her, as Ken Blanchard so aptly states, "A goal is a dream with wings." In order to accomplish this goal, she focused on what needed to be done and never lost sight of the end point. Like most of us, she ran into obstacles along the way, but she never lost focus.

Be Counted

Set the example for others and be strong when the situation demands it. When the chips were down and her friends were being intimidated, Dorothy stepped to the front and confronted the Wizard. She knew that she had to stand up and be counted. In doing this she gained the admiration of everyone involved.

It's Okay to Show Emotion

Many of us are taught from early childhood that "big boys" don't cry. Bull! When you show emotion, it lets people know you're real, that you have feelings and that you care. And when people know that you care about them they will move mountains for you.

Peaks and Valleys

Life is a series of peaks and valleys, and unfortunately, there are no bridges to take us from peak to peak. We have to go down in the valley to get to the next peak. However, when you're "down" in the valley remember how wonderful the view was at the peak.

Follow your yellow brick road to success in the new millennium. Get to know all of those you meet, talk with them, help them, and let them know you care. If you do, like Dorothy, you'll reach your final destination.

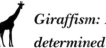 *Giraffism: Like Dorothy, we must be strongly determined and have a heart of gold.*

JUST "PLANE CRAZY"
Southwest Airlines Employees Are "Nuts" about their Business

One of the best selling business books in recent years is entitled, *Nuts! Southwest Airlines' Crazy Recipe for Business and Personal Success.* The book was written by Kevin and Jackie Freiberg and tells the story of a company that makes money, is the most productive in the airline industry, has the lowest turnover rate of employees, has never had a layoff, and whose employees have fun at what they do.

It's the story of a company whose founder dressed up as Corporal Klinger, a sheik, and Elvis—to name a few—at company functions and who arm wrestled the chairman of another company instead of going to court over an advertising slogan. It's a great story and a lesson for all of us. It's the story of a company that dares to be different, encourages and instills leadership in every nook and cranny of the organization, and is serious about its core values.

Kevin Freiberg was the keynote speaker at the Virginia Forum for Excellence, a forum that attracts 700-800 business leaders. His presentation was fantastic and afterwards I spent the remainder of the day with him talking about organizations, success, leadership, and customer service. As president of the San Diego Consulting Group, Kevin has worked with many leading organizations throughout the United States. He has consulted with Southwest Airlines for over 10 years and shared many reasons for their success. What an education and what a learning experience!

Kevin shared why Southwest is the only airline that has made money for the last 30 years. He shared why 137,000 job applicants applied for 5,000 jobs when the pay is about the same at other airlines. He related that their employees take ownership and pride in everything they do.

Hire People Who Care

First and foremost, Southwest hires for attitude and trains for skills. They are a firm believer that you hire fun, unselfish people who are committed to doing whatever it takes to get the job done. Just think about it. You can't teach attitude, but you can teach skills. That doesn't mean that if you need an accountant, you hire someone who can't add and subtract. It does mean, however, that you find the most qualified person you can who is passionate about the organization and what they do. Hire people who do what they love, love what they do, and who don't take themselves too seriously.

Color Outside the Lines

One of the things that Southwest encourages is for their employees to "color outside the lines." They want their people to come up with new and dynamic ways to meet customer needs. Their management team understands that creative, entrusted teammates bend, stretch or break the rules that don't serve the customer's needs. When people feel like they are "owners" of a business they take a great interest, become cost-conscious, industrious, and imaginative.

Celebrate Everything

Southwest takes every opportunity to celebrate their successes. They honor individual groups, significant events and important accomplishments in many different and creative ways. In doing this they understand that celebrations "charge up" and inspire people, build their relationships, create memories, acknowledge what is important and keep spirits high. They have truly taken celebrations to a new level.

Your organization, too, can fly sky high, soar with the best, and reach new heights. Just take a lesson from those "plane crazy" people at Southwest Airlines. After all, they're just "nuts" about being the best.

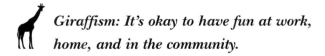 *Giraffism: It's okay to have fun at work, home, and in the community.*

AIN'T NO MOUNTAIN HIGH ENOUGH
Climbing the Ladder of Success

Afew years ago (I like to think of it that way) one of the hottest and best-selling records in the country was a song by Marvin Gaye entitled "Ain't No Mountain High Enough." For those of you who strive to climb the ladder of success in both your professional and personal lives, adopting this song title would be a great theme to live by.

In our personal and professional lives, high achievers are always climbing new mountains, seeking new challenges and coming up with creative and better ways to accomplish goals. So, if you think of a mountain as never being high enough, you will constantly be motivated to do whatever it takes to accomplish any task that comes your way.

Successful Climbers

Who are the successful mountain climbers and what characteristics must they possess? First of all, successful mountain climbers are determined individuals. They put their nose to the grindstone and are willing to do whatever it takes to get the job done. The words "I can't do it" are not part of their vocabulary. Rather, they echo the thoughts of Winston Churchill when asked to address the graduating class at one of England's most prestigious preparatory schools. The students were expecting a long and winded speech. Sir Winston's entire address was simply, "Never give in. Never, Never, Never!"

Resilience Is Key

Resilience is another key characteristic of individuals striving to reach new heights. They know that they will encounter many obstacles, but they also know they will be able to overcome whatever challenges these obstacles present. Many salespeople fail because they can't accept the rejection of not making the sale. They feel defeated and take it personally. I've never met a salesperson who made a sale on every call. I know of many who set that as their goal and rightly so. And if they didn't make the sale, their attitude was, "I'll get you the next time." Just think of it as another mountain to successfully climb.

Work!

Successful mountain climbers work smart and hard. They don't waste energy, but they give it their all. They fully understand that their leadership and perspiration will be an inspiration to others.

Markel Corporation is a great example of a company that has climbed the ladder of success and who is an inspiration to others.

With "roots" dating back to the '20s, Markel has become a giant in the insurance industry with assets exceeding $5 billion. Their secret? Hard work, innovation and the "Markel Style" that focuses on looking for new and better ways to serve its customers.

It's All about Attitude

Attitude will determine your altitude! If you think you can't, you won't. If you think you can, you will! Ninety percent of what you accomplish in life can be attributed to your attitude.

The late, great Norman Vincent Peale, minister of New York City's Marble Collegiate Church and famous author, preached for over 70 years about the importance of attitude in everything you do. In his best-selling books, *The Power Of Positive Thinking* and *Enthusiasm Makes The Difference,* Dr. Peale talks about the fact that we become what we think. He also stresses to never forget that all of the enthusiasm you need is in your mind. Let it out—let it live—let it motivate you. William James, one of the wisest men that America has ever produced, stated it best when he said, "The greatest discovery of my generation is that human beings can alter their lives by altering their attitudes of mind."

 Giraffism: To climb the ladder of success, always set your sights on the highest mountain you can find…and climb it!

THE SERVICE GENERATION—HITTING THE SPOT

"Pepsi-Cola hits the spot
12 full ounces that's a lot
All of this for a nickel too
Pepsi-Cola is the
drink for you."

As a young boy growing up, the above jingle from Pepsi was one that was constantly played on every radio station. (We had no TV.) The ad had a catchy tune, and I must have heard it thousands of times and it greatly influenced my soft drink selection in those days. Pepsi has continued its appeal to the young with their on-going series of Pepsi Generation ads.

Likewise, companies that understand service excellence believe they are part of the Service Generation. This generation has its own jingle and is committed to providing superior service, as they know it is key to their success.

When you visit or talk with the companies that are true champions of customer satisfaction, you can't help but be impressed with the quality of the processes they have established and the way they relate to their employees.

First Impressions

For those companies that are really "into it" it is obvious to everyone. One of the first indications is the way visitors and employees are greeted by the receptionists, either in person or over the phone. These receptionists have smiles in their voices and one senses immediately that they love what they do and do what they love. They are pleasant, caring, responsible individuals who set the tone for their organization. I'm sure you've visited many organizations where you were greeted by "Oscar the Grouch" or "Scrooge." It appears that they work hard at being difficult, grumpy, rude and unpleasant. And it is hard work because it takes only three muscles to smile and 66 to frown. Talk about wasted energy.

There is no doubt that first impressions are lasting ones, and companies that excel at service excellence coach and talk with their employees. Their process of first impressions begins in the hiring process. In hiring, they look for people who have a spirit to serve, who like people, who have fun, and who genuinely want to help. They look for people who take pride in their appearance, who have a positive attitude and who think that the phrase "It can't be done" is from an alien planet.

Common Sense Makes Sense

Companies that excel at service excellence use common sense as their *modus operandi*. They stay away from sophisticated "programs" that get their people so wrapped up in the process they forget that the main purpose of any service process is to serve the customer. They stress the basics and appeal to the "human" side of humans. They talk "with" and not "to" their employees and communicate with them at every level. They want their employees to feel "in" on things, as they know a happy employee is a productive employee.

Red Robin Sings Its Song

An example of a company that lives this philosophy is Red Robin Inns. They keep their people informed and provide them with the training and tools to satisfy their guests. Their motto simply states that, "A Happy Guest is Our Success." They ask their employees to practice the following five things with their guests:

1. Look at them.
2. Smile at them.
3. Talk to them.
4. Listen to them.
5. Thank them.

Really Sophisticated Stuff!

Likewise, Malcom Baldridge National Quality Award-recipient Ritz-Carlton Hotels utilize the same approach. They keep things simple, consistent, pleasant and task-oriented. They also entrust their employees to carry out their philosophy. Each employee carries a small (2⅛" x 3⅞") laminated card. The front of the card simply states, "We are ladies and gentlemen serving ladies and gentlemen." Inside the card are three basic steps of service:

> A warm and sincere greeting. Use the
> guest's name if and when possible.
> Anticipation and compliance with
> guest needs.
> Fond Farewell. Give them a warm
> goodbye and use their names if
> and when possible.

Pretty simple, but most effective.

Make the commitment to be a part of the "Service Generation" and generate warmth, good will, trust and superior service to everyone involved. Be there for your customers and understand that they pay your salaries. Create your own "service" jingle and make sure you "hit the spot" with your customers.

 Giraffism: Customer service is all about treating others the way they want to be treated.

ARE YOU A RAPTOR OR MENTOR?

Millions of years ago, raptors and other dinosaurs roamed the earth. They were dominant, terrifying, and caused much destruction. When I asked my step-children, Amanda and Sam, about raptors, they gave me lots of information. First, they mentioned that raptors were known as birds of prey that included a night-hunting order as well as a day-hunting order. These raptors all had sharp bills and curved, sharp claws. The claws were on both their hands and feet and they used them to harm others. They looked mean and resembled what we know today as vultures.

Picture these dinosaurs in your mind. They look scary, feed off of the misfortune of others, inflict pain, and tend to show satisfaction when they cause disruption. Their very nature is to be destructive. They don't want to build anything; they want to tear it apart or down.

Now, even though dinosaurs have supposedly been extinct for years, they exist in our world today. We see them at work, at church, and in the communities where we live. People fail to grow, develop and feel good about themselves because of dinosaurs who refuse to give direction and encouragement and who continually spout negative thoughts.

Successful companies have worked very hard to eliminate their dinosaurs and replace them with caring, competent individuals. They select individuals who truly want to help others and who pose the question, "What can I do to help you succeed?" These companies understand that leaders develop leaders, and they place the kind of individuals in leadership positions that can move the company forward.

Servant Leader/Mentor

The best leaders/mentors I have ever met are servant leaders/mentors. They help people remove obstacles that face them and help them acquire the tools they need to do their jobs better. They understand the coach's role and the value of coaching. Great coaches are fair and firm but they are also kind, caring and patient individuals. When needed, they are willing to jump into the trenches and do whatever they ask of others. They are faithful servants to the people they lead, and they share in their victories and defeats. They know they can't do the job for the other person, but they clearly understand they can use their savvy, knowledge and experience to help others succeed.

Mentors Develop Mentors

In helping others, great mentors have as one of their goals to develop mentors. While raptors are caustic and destructive, mentors are supportive and positive.

Years ago when I worked at Squibb Corporation, one of my mentors was a gentleman by the name of Andy Anderson. Andy was vice president of sales, and one of the best speakers I've ever had the privilege of hearing. I was asked to give a speech to all of Squibb's regional and division managers and I thought I was prepared. Being the good mentor that he was, Andy made me go through a dry run the day before. About halfway through the speech he stopped me and pulled me aside. It was obvious to him that I was not prepared and not at my best. Instead of pointing out my negatives, and there were many, he simply stated, "Goldie, I want you to be perceived as a great speaker, but to be that, you need to work on certain parts of your speech and practice, practice, practice." (Talk about inspect what you expect!) He concluded with, "I like you too much to have you being perceived as someone who's not at the top of his game." I've never forgotten his words, but more importantly, the way he took time to help me be the best that I could be.

Are you taking time to help others? Are you letting them know you care? Do you have as your goal to make a difference in their lives? If you can answer "yes" to all of these questions, you'll never take the "rap" for being a raptor. And for all of our sakes, the only good raptors are those that you find in the Smithsonian.

 Giraffism: Great mentors take an interest in and make a difference in the lives of others.

DON'T SETTLE FOR LESS

One of the most catchy advertising jingles of all time was the U.S. Army's, "Be All That You Can Be." The advertisement encourages you to be adventurous, do things you've never done, reach for new heights, believe in yourself, develop your potential, and live your life to the fullest.

Being the best is a lifetime job and great leaders—and organizations—push themselves to be better, faster and smarter than their competition. There are too many organizations and leaders who feel they "know it all" and are too old and well established to learn.

What does one need to do? What does it take to develop one's potential and, more importantly, stay at the top of one's game?

Challenge Yourself

The first step is to always challenge yourself to seek the new. The most successful people I know are those who are looking for new and better ways to do things. They know there's a better mousetrap out there and they want to build it.

Have a Plan

To be all you can be requires having a plan. If you were planning a trip to California, one of the first things you would do is to secure a road map. The map would help you plan the most expedient and efficient way to reach your destination. The same holds true for success in business and life. Take time to think about and map out your strategies. Set priorities and follow them.

Be Competitive

Great organizations and leaders have a will to win—they realize that no one ever remembers who finished second. They know the great feeling that comes in being a winner and once they experience that feeling, it's always there. In winning, they understand the importance of keeping score and of always knowing where one stands. They know that to be competitive they must always "raise the bar" and show improvement in areas essential to their success.

Never Give In

As mentioned in an earlier chapter, one of the great mentors in my life was Norman Vincent Peale, pastor of Marble Collegiate Church in New York and author of the best-selling book, *The Power Of Positive Thinking.* As I sat in church and listened to Dr. Peale, he continually reinforced the fact that the only limitations we have are those that we place on ourselves. If we feel we can't get it done, we won't. On the other hand, if we approach every situation with an "I can do it" attitude, we will.

Self Improvement

Great leaders and organizations are always looking for ways to improve. They are also quick to change things if they are not working. They look at other people and organizations and "borrow" the things those people and organizations do better. Go into a K-Mart or a Target store and you'll see the things that have made Wal*Mart a $190 billion-plus company. Imitation is the sincerest form of flattery, and there's nothing wrong in implementing programs and policies that have worked for others.

Be Gutsy

Last but certainly not least, one has to be gutsy and try new and even unorthodox approaches. If what you're doing isn't working, seek the new. Dare to be different.

Make a commitment to "be all that you can be." Be the "captain" in charge and make a "major" difference in your life and in the lives of others.

 Giraffism: Being the best is a lifetime job.

CELEBRATE YOUR SUCCESSES
Be A Winner!

"Celebrate your successes. Find some humor in your failures. Don't take yourself so seriously. Loosen up and everyone around you will loosen up.

"Have fun. Show enthusiasm always. When all else fails, put on a costume and sing a silly song. Then have everybody else sing with you." These words, spoken by Wal*Mart founder, Sam Walton, are so important to one's success. When people celebrate their successes, it means that they have won, and there is no greater feeling than that of a winner.

So, what do you do to celebrate? Perhaps it's going out to dinner, playing golf or tennis, going to a movie or buying a book. Personally I buy neckties. (I now own three.)

Listening and Responding Creates Success

Before you celebrate your successes, you must be successful. And what does it take to be successful? First and foremost, you must service your customers. Successful salespeople make the customer number one. They work for their customers and know that the customer signs their paychecks.

Successful salespeople are responsive to their customers' needs and practice the philosophy that response time should be in minutes, not hours. Most of all, they listen to what their customers are saying and ask, "What can I do to help you succeed?"

Next, successful salespeople exceed their customers' expectations. Customers expect you to keep your word. Exceed it!

Nordstrom; Southwest Airlines; Federal Express; Ritz-Carlton; Disney; Ukrop's; Henrico County, Virginia, school system; and Owens&Minor consistently exceed their customers' expectations. They do this by listening to their customers' needs and developing strategies to ensure satisfaction.

Tend to the Details

Commit to excellence. There is an old saying that "little things mean a lot." That's wrong. Little things mean everything!

Communicate, communicate, communicate. How successful you might be depends on your communication skills. The best communicators are the best listeners, not the best talkers. When you communicate, be honest and open. Involve your customers in the conversation. Feedback is the breakfast of champions and your customers will provide you a road map to the future.

Exude Energy and Enthusiasm

Energize others. People love to deal with people who are positive and enthusiastic. Infect them with your enthusiasm.

Remember that people are persuaded by reason, but moved by emotion. Your attitude will affect your altitude and the only limits to how far you can climb are self-imposed.

Share your successes with your teammates. When you do this, you become a learning organization and when you share, everyone benefits. Work together as a team, knowing that together, everyone achieves more.

Sincerity Leads to Great Things

Last but not least, be sincere with your customers. We've all heard of the KISS method, which reads, "Keep It Simple, Stupid." I prefer to substitute the phrase "and sincere" for stupid. When you're sincere, people know that you have their best interests at heart. You gain their trust, admiration and respect.

So, be a winner and celebrate your successes, whether big or small. Not only will it focus you on your accomplishments but you will feel so good about yourself and what you've done, the word "winner" will have a great resonance to it!

 Giraffism: Take time to smell the flowers and "flower" those around you.

DARE TO BE DIFFERENT

He looked different. At six feet four inches and 180 pounds, he was kind of gawky. He was slightly stooped, had unruly hair, wore a shabby old top hat, a bad-fitting frock coat and pantaloons, and un-blackened boots.

He came from poor beginnings, was culturally unsophisticated, and lacked administrative and diplomatic skills.

He was one of the most maligned of the American presidents and yet he is recognized as one of the top five presidents in United States history.

What made this man from the mountains of Kentucky so special? Why did he succeed where others failed? Why was he admired and loved by the public?

The answer is simple. He dared to be different. He thought outside the box. He wasn't afraid to make tough decisions, decisions that sometimes rendered him unpopular. He spoke his mind and shared his feelings, but did so in a most positive, caring manner.

Believe in Yourself

If people are to be different, they have to believe in themselves and their abilities. They must stick by their guns and never waver like a twig in the wind. They must accept the fact that they can't please everyone, but take solace in knowing that they are honest and fair in dealing with others. The perception of "Honest Abe" was that he was the people's president, that he was straightforward and above all, honest.

People who believe in themselves deal from a position of strength. They know they can get the job done, but they don't waste time telling others that they can. Their actions speak louder than their words and because of this they are an inspiration to others. They "walk the talk" and don't ask others to do things they wouldn't do.

Reason and Emotion

One of the things that great leaders are not afraid to do is show their emotions. People are persuaded by reason, but moved by emotion. Big boys don't cry is an oxymoron, as all of the great leaders I know are not afraid to laugh or cry! Great leaders show emotion. People know when great leaders are happy or disappointed. Sam Walton was a consistent cheerleader for his Wal*Mart teammates, however he didn't hesitate to let them know when he was disappointed with their service or performance. The same holds true for Herb Kelleher, founder of Southwest Airlines. On Thanksgiving eve, the busiest day in the airline industry, you would find Herb working with and encouraging his baggage handlers at Love Field in Dallas. I'm sure you can imagine the positive effect this has on his workers.

On the other side of the coin, it gave him an opportunity to observe his employees' performance. Southwest has a reputation for having the best turnaround time in the industry. From the time a plane lands, unloads its passengers and cargo, and loads its new passengers and cargo, it takes 20 minutes; the average for the airline industry is 40! By working with his people, Herb got a good sense of how they were doing the job. If they weren't, he didn't hesitate to find someone who could.

Be Yourself

The best advice I ever received in my life was from a great friend and mentor, Mike Bongiovanni, the president for E.R. Squibb & Sons. Mike was a great leader and mentor who refused to let those around him fail. As an Italian immigrant and an Horatio Alger Award winner, he knew what it took to overcome obstacles and be successful. When he saw that people were going astray, he'd sit with them and remind them to do those things that had made them successful. He'd also remind them to use their strengths to try things differently, to be an innovator, and to think outside the box. He'd always say, "Dare to be different."

Abe Lincoln had a different look, and a different view and perspective. And all it did for him was have him recognized as one of the most respected presidents this country has ever produced.

 Giraffism: Be yourself and seek the new.

Are You Pushing or Pulling the Rubber Band?

If you look at most successful sales and marketing companies, or at any company for that matter, they are noted for their exceptional leadership. Leaders can and do make a difference. Because leaders know their own minds, are visionary and possess a great deal of self-confidence, they inspire others to excel and to reach new heights.

Good leaders know that "You can lead a horse to water, but you can't make the horse drink." Thus, they create an atmosphere or environment that is based upon the fact that people count, are needed and make a difference.

They know that leadership is an art and, like most great artists, they must practice, practice and practice. One doesn't become a great leader by reading a book, going to a seminar, or listening to a tape.

True leaders are effective communicators who possess good old common sense and who make sound, non-political decisions. They are stewards and servants to their people and they give them room to grow.

They know that the old way of "you do it my way or else" has gone the way of the dinosaur and that they must take care, be sensitive to and understand their employees' needs.

One of the best ways to vividly demonstrate what leadership is all about is by using a rubber band. Break the rubber band, place it on a table and push it. Watch what happens. The rubber band goes in circles, knots up and doesn't do anything you want. On the other hand, take the same rubber band and pull it. Note that the rubber band follows exactly the way you're pulling it. Pulling people along is what leadership is all about and when you pull them, they understand you're supporting and "pulling for" them.

Great leaders inspire their followers. People are persuaded by reason but moved by emotion, and the leader must both persuade and move them. The leader must also have the best interests of their followers at heart. Someone once asked, "What's the difference between a manager and a leader?" The answer given was, "Managers have as their goal to do things right; leaders have as their goal to do the right thing." And there's one heck of a difference in doing things right versus doing the right thing!

Mortimer Feinberg, the great industrial psychologist, and author of *Why Smart People Do Dumb Things*, once told me that to be a good leader one must be a dreamer, reamer, schemer and healer. Of those four characteristics, dreaming accounts for 20% of your time, reaming 2%, scheming 3% and healing 75%.

Great leaders dream about the future and think of new ways to do things better. They are committed to getting things done.

An effective leader must also be a reamer and that is not one of the more pleasant duties they perform. In being a reamer, leaders are firm but fair. They know it's not what you say, but how you say it that counts.

In terms of scheming—honest scheming that is—leaders think of creative and innovative ways to inspire and motivate people to meet and beat the challenges that face them. A good leader "feels" for his/her people and tailors a plan to help them develop their full potential. Last, but certainly not least, leaders constantly "heal" their people. They let them know that it's okay to make a mistake and they themselves admit to their own mistakes.

Leaders let the person save face at all costs. They catch their people doing the right things and let them know how much they are appreciated. Most of all, leaders recognize and reward achievement, letting their people know that they genuinely care about them.

One final thought. If you're a good leader, your team has confidence in you. If you are a great leader, they have confidence in themselves.

There's a lot to being a good leader. It is not something to take lightly as our future depends on the leader's ability to communicate, inspire and develop others. Are you that leader?

 Giraffism: When you "pull" people along they feel you're supporting and pulling for them.

AIN'T NONE OF US AS GOOD AS ALL OF US

One of the words we hear thrown around loosely is the word "team" or "teamwork." We hear companies proclaim that they are a team or that teamwork is the order of the day. We hear "together we can make a difference" or "there is no 'I' in team" or "together everyone achieves more." These are magnificent words and slogans, but unfortunately in most companies, that's all they are.

I recently was in St. Louis talking with newspaper people from all across the country. There were individuals from *The Washington Post, The Philadelphia Enquirer, The Miami Herald, The St. Louis Post-Dispatch, The Baltimore Sun,* and the list goes on and on. One of the complaints focused on the fact that their organization didn't operate as a team. They felt that they were disjointed and that management didn't care or listen.

Their complaints and feelings are not exclusive to the newspaper industry. You find the same thoughts and feelings in companies throughout the U.S. What always puzzles me is that many of these companies are struggling to make a profit, and yet they fail to comprehend that the way you treat your people is the way they treat your customers. They also don't realize that happy employees are productive employees who will go the extra mile because they know management cares.

Walk the Talk

Look at America's most successful organizations and you'll find a pattern. The leaders in these companies don't expect their people to do anything they wouldn't do. Colleen Barrett of Southwest Airlines, Jim and Bobby Ukrop of Ukrop's Super Markets, Bernie Marcus of Home Depot and Gil Minor of Owens&Minor meet regularly with their employees to listen to what they have to say. These CEOs know they are the team leaders and that they must set the example for others to follow.

One for All and All for One

The Three Musketeers knew what they were talking about when they uttered the phrase, "One for all and all for one." What that simply means is that we are all in this together, and by sharing and helping each other, we'll succeed. Put another way, we are all each other's customers. True, some of us bring more to the table than others, but that's okay. What each of us individually brings contributes to the success of the organization. If one of us thinks we're bigger than all of us, we're in trouble as a team.

Team Talk

One of the greatest ways to ensure that you function as a team is to communicate everything you possibly can. Great teams understand that you can't over-communicate good information. Make sure everyone has their say in the matter as it makes them feel like they are wanted or needed. I was watching a YMCA ten-year-old league basketball game and on one team there were two prima donnas, or what I call ball hogs. They didn't want to pass the ball to anybody except each other. The other three members on the floor felt left out, frustrated and downtrodden. You could see it in their faces and overall body language. They wanted desperately to be a part of the team and contribute. The same holds true for any team you put together, whether it's a family, community, business or church team. By the way—the two ball hogs scored 20 points. Unfortunately, the other "team" scored 40!

Make it a goal to be a team player and to encourage everyone to participate. Team-up to make a difference, to raise the bar and to soar to new heights. 'Cause you see, it makes no difference how good you are, you can't do it alone.

 Giraffism: There are three letters in the word "one" and four in the word "team"... advantage team.

BE COOL

Irecently had the pleasure of talking with 50 young people from the Burger King Academy in Chesterfield County, Virginia. They had spent the morning shadowing employees who work for the county. It was a great feeling to be with them.

On my way to meeting these youngsters I mulled over the kind of message I should share with them. I wanted to deliver a message they could relate to, one that I hoped would inspire them, and one that they could draw from as they made their way in life.

I finally decided to talk with them about being "cool," but not in the conventional sense. My message was based on what being cool really means to employers. To illustrate my point, I utilize the letters in the word "cool."

"C" is for "Communication"

Earl Nightingale, the old sales motivator, once said, "The effectiveness of one's life is determined by the effectiveness of one's communication skills."

It's important that all of us learn to become better communicators, which also means becoming a better listener. Once we learn to listen we know more about people—their likes, dislikes, interests, and what makes them tick.

You want to make sure you talk WITH and not TO people. There's only a two-letter difference between the four-letter word "with" and the two-letter word "to," but what a huge difference. When you talk to people you put them at arm's length. When you talk with others, they are with you.

"O" is for "On the Ball"

We've all heard that the Marines are looking for a few good men and women. Guess what? Companies are looking for lots of good people. People that care. People that seek the new. People that take pride in everything they do. At Owens&Minor we are always looking for teammates who will take the ball and run with it. We want teammates who don't have the word "average" in their vocabulary. To us, average is where the best of the worst meets the worst of the best. We want teammates who are never satisfied with meeting expectations, but elated when they exceed them.

"O" is for "Ownership"

Being "cool" means taking ownership. When you are assigned a job or project, it's key that you are accountable and responsible for all aspects of the project. One of the buzzwords in business today is empowerment. All empowerment is, really, is owning what is assigned to you and taking the appropriate actions to make sure things come to fruition. When you own a project, you believe in it and do what it takes to make sure it's completed on time. Think about it! When you own something, you go to great lengths to care for it. It's yours and that's a great feeling. Ownership is all about pride, passion and caring.

"L" is for "Love What You Do"

If you love what you do and do what you love, you'll be a success. When it becomes a chore to go to work or you come home mad every day, it's time to look for something else. Happy people are productive people and they see the fruits of their efforts.

So if you want to be known as someone who's pretty cool, learn to communicate like crazy, don't be satisfied with the status quo, be responsible and accountable, and love and have fun at what you do. It's a known fact that people who love what they do are highly motivated by their own enthusiasm, which in turn drives them to continually raise the bar. Unhappy people wallow in one disappointment after another, always seeking the elusive silver bullet. They try to manufacture happiness, but that is an impossible task. Happiness is a natural resource, and when you love what you do, it shows.

 Giraffism: "Cool" people don't worry about being in the hot seat.

ARE YOU PUTTING PEOPLE FIRST?

Quality organizations are always redefining, redesigning, or, in plain simple English, redoing their quality/continuous improvement/customer service processes.

At Owens&Minor, we have redefined our quality processes and the words we use to recognize and re-ignite our teammates are "Putting People First."

It's a catchy and meaningful phrase and I'd like to take credit for it. However, the credit belongs to Ann Greer Rector, a former chief financial officer (CFO) at Owens&Minor who died unexpectedly.

Ann Greer Rector was a brilliant, gallant lady who not only knew the value of the numbers, but the value that people bring to the table. In a world where the bottom line is everything to most, Ann realized that the bottom line is only as good as the people who contribute their many talents and energies to making the bottom line tops.

What a spectacular lady, and one who made a difference in the lives of all of us at Owens&Minor. We miss her, but we are all better people because our paths crossed.

Making a Difference

You, too, can make a difference with your friends, relatives, children and teammates if you put them first. My friend Jackie Freiberg, co-author of the top-selling business book, *NUTS!*, says it best when she asks companies and individuals to choose service over self-interest. That's a powerful statement and one that we should all follow.

We hear the phrase "servant leaders" and the difference they make in the lives of others. Servant leaders aren't worried about status, the title on their business card, or the sign on their door. They are interested in their teammates and what they can do to help them succeed. Servant leaders don't take themselves too seriously. They know that the more they give the more they get in return. They understand the value of putting people first.

Put Your People First

What is putting people first all about? First and foremost, it's all about letting people know that you care about them. When people know that you care, they become over-achievers. Mark Edwards, Superintendant of Schools, Henrico County, Virginia, is great at putting people first and cheering them on. His leadership skills have made him one of the most sought out educators in the United States.

We all like to feel wanted and needed. It makes us feel good when people recognize and pay attention to us. We smile and feel elated inside, and when we smile it automatically relaxes us. It takes 66 muscles to frown and only three muscles to smile. That being the case, why would we want to waste all that energy frowning?

Communicate Like Crazy

When you put your people first, you routinely keep them informed. Recent surveys indicate that the number one thing people want most from their jobs is feeling in on things. None of us likes to be kept in the dark. It makes us feel unimportant and unwanted. Let people know what's going on in the organization, what they can expect and how they can influence issues. At Owens&Minor we have a hard and fast rule that team leaders hold monthly meetings with their teams and weekly meetings with their direct reports. You cannot over-communicate accurate information. When you do communicate, keep it simple and to the point. Keep your meetings and your memos short.

Putting People First? It's what successful organizations and successful leaders do. There's no greater feeling than feeling like and being a winner. And guess what? Winners finish "first."

 Giraffism: One of the first rules of business is to put your employees first. If you do, they'll do the same for your business.

Carbon Paper Doesn't Last Very Long

Back in the dark ages, before the advent of the copier, fax machine, and home printers, people used carbon paper or carbon sets to make copies. One could buy a box of carbon paper for a small pittance. And you needed to buy a box because after being used for a short period of time one piece would wear thin or wear out. Plus, it never had the look of the original.

There's a lesson to be learned for all of us in this. When we try to emulate or copy others, we, too, wear thin or wear out.

Each and every one of us has our own uniqueness, personality, traits and quirks that separate us from others. The people that I've met over the years who try to be something they are not, ARE NOT. When we try to imitate others, we inevitably fail.

No One Like You

I remember when I was climbing the corporate ladder at Squibb Corporation. I was sent to an industrial psychologist who was going to mold me into another Harold Geneen (former head of ITT). He was to be my "personal" coach.

The first time we met he asked me to give a fifteen-minute speech on any subject. As I spoke he taped it and afterwards critiqued what

I had done right and what I had done wrong. I remember his critique to this day. He told me I was too animated, too enthusiastic, and that I must pause after each sentence. He pointed out that Harold Geneen never smiled when he spoke and that's what it took to become CEO of a Fortune 500 company. So being kind of naïve and dumb at that young age, I decided to try it out on my wife that night. Her first reaction was that I'd had a stroke, was having a stroke, or some weird reaction to a drug a physician had given me. It wasn't me (or anybody else for that matter) and I was terrible. It taught me a great lesson, however, and to this day I've always made it a point to be myself.

Learn from Others

The one thing we can do, however, is learn from others. Great leaders find out what works and incorporate it into their style. They know they can't do it the way others do, nor do they want to. However, they are never too proud to learn from others. They learn what to do as well as what not to do.

Be Yourself

Years ago I heard Norman Vincent Peale preach a sermon entitled, "Be Yourself." In his sermon he talked about the fact that if you traveled the whole world over, you'd never find another person like yourself. He stated that a genetic scientist had said that if you had 300 billion brothers and sisters, none of them would be exactly like you.

What Dr. Peale was pointing out is that we are all unique and that we must use our talents to the best of our abilities. Some of us have more talents and abilities than others. But that's okay! What we must do is utilize the talents we have in our own inimitable style. Key in all of this is that we know ourselves, our strengths, our limitations, and how we can make a difference.

Try Something New

Don't be afraid to try new and different things. Trying new and different things doesn't mean you have to imitate or be someone else. In an earlier chapter, I pointed out that Abraham Lincoln dared to be different. He met many obstacles and hazards on his way to becoming one of our greatest presidents. He was unique looking and different than others, but he believed in his abilities, and more importantly, in himself. He knew inside that he could be one of the best presidents, ever!

Don't be a carbon copy of anyone. If you try to be, like carbon paper, you, too, will eventually fade and wear thin.

 Giraffism: Being different can make the difference.

SWING THE BAT

In watching the World Series between the New York Yankees and Atlanta Braves, I was amazed at the number of batters who stood at the plate and "took" pitches.

Instead of swinging the bat, they watched as pitcher after pitcher threw accurate strikes across the plate. Even when the "count" was zero balls and two strikes, their bats remained on their shoulders. In most cases they were counted out without ever taking any swings at all.

Observing this reminded me of many people that I see in my travels and everyday activities. They go through life without ever swinging the bat, being complacent and taking what comes along. They just watch things happen as opposed to making things happen, and because of it, success comes hard for them.

On the other hand, there are those who make things happen, who are not satisfied with the status quo, and who are committed to making a difference. They thrive when the pressure is on, and their energy and enthusiasm are contagious to all they touch. They are doers who know they must stand up and be counted.

Every Minute Counts

There's an old adage that if you want something done, get a busy person to do it. Now that sounds a little strange because common sense tells you one should get someone who is not busy. However, busy people are doers and extremely organized. They make great use of time and are great delegators. They also understand that all work and no play makes one a very dull person. They balance their time between their families, work and community and have fun doing all three. They are very much into and practice the philosophy, "If it ain't fun, it don't get done."

One of the best leaders I have ever met at making every minute count is Jim Dunn, President of the Greater Richmond Chamber of Commerce. Jim is a brilliant, organized individual who can juggle many balls at one time. He does this, however, in a most professional, competent, and easy going manner. And it's obvious he has fun doing it.

Count to Ten (in Spanish!)

Be prepared to do new things. Think of new and better ways to do things differently. The most successful people I know are those who can change and/or adapt to change. If you become satisfied with the status quo, that is exactly what you get. Read new books, learn a new language, or learn all you can about the Internet. Be creative, imaginative, and most of all seek the new.

Don't Be a "Count" Dracula

If you are going to be successful in the new millennium, make it a goal to be a servant leader. There are too many Count Draculas in the workplace who inflict pain and drain the life out of others.

Servant leaders lead from the heart. To them, life is all about people getting A's. When people get C's, it concerns them, and their response to those who are struggling is, "What can I do to help you succeed?" They thrive on making potential winners, WINNERS!

Servant leaders have genuine humility but tons of confidence. In their book, *Leadership by the Book,* Ken Blanchard, Bill Hybels and Phil Hodges state it best; servant leaders "don't think less of themselves, they just think about themselves less."

To servant leaders, personal power, recognition or money are never at the forefront. They love to help others succeed. They always want to be held accountable because they want to know if they are making a difference. If not, they will take whatever actions are necessary to make sure they do. They enhance others' lives and know that Count Dracula is just what he should be—a fictitious character.

Make it a personal goal to let others know that you'll come out "swinging" and that they can count on you. If you do, you'll be a "hit" to those you touch.

 Giraffism: In the game of life, don't be a spectator.

It's in the Bag

Ukrop's Super Markets, Inc. has been in business for over 65 years. During this time they have built customer loyalty to where today they have a 43% share of the grocery store business in their area. That's unheard of in the grocery store market and a remarkable feat.

The first question that should come to your mind is: What did they do to achieve this status? How do they differ from their competitors?

To start with, they bag your groceries and take them to your car. There is no tipping involved, as it is one of the many services they provide. This seems like such a small thing, but it's something that looms big in the minds of its customers. Ukrop's is a master at taking care of the little things.

Next, if you're looking for an item in any of their 28 stores, one of their associates will walk with you to where the product is located. There's no pointing fingers or drawing maps as to where to go. Another little thing.

Third, they hire people who love to work with people, and they put them through an extensive and continuous training program. No new associate can work on the floor until they attend Healthy Start, their orientation program.

Once they train their associates, they entrust them to think on their feet and make decisions. There is not someone peering over one's shoulder trying to catch people making errors. They encourage their associates to make suggestions that they feel will make Ukrop's a better place to work.

Recognition, Reinforcement and Reward

Recognition, reinforcement and reward are a big part of their success. When an associate celebrates a birthday, they receive a card and $50 and are given the day off. These cards are individually signed by Jim Ukrop, Chairman of the Board, and Bobby Ukrop, CEO and President. It's also not uncommon to see these two brothers in their stores at all hours of the day thanking associates for doing a good job and even bagging groceries. Both are very approachable and always take time to listen to their associates.

Once a year there is a company picnic where food, games and camaraderie is the order of the day. Special awards and citations are presented at this picnic which enhances and perpetuates the team concept.

Associates wear polo-type shirts that proclaim loudly on the chest TEAM UKROP'S. They understand the value of teammates taking pride in their work and organization.

Community Involvement

Ukrop's associates are very active in the community working with projects that involve people of all ages who need help. It's a great way to practice teamwork out of the normal work environment and get associates to know each other better.

A prime example of this is the Ukrop's Christmas Parade, held the first Saturday in December each year. It is the largest parade in Virginia. Associates decorate floats, carry helium-filled balloons in the parade, and help organize the event.

Treat People Well

Jim and Bobby Ukrop understand that if they take care of their associates, their associates will take care of them. They have a reputation for being fair to all concerned and they work diligently to keep their associates feeling good about themselves. They understand that happy people are productive people who take pride in everything they do.

For the Ukrops, customer satisfaction and profits are truly in the bag.

 Giraffism: If you don't treat your employees well, you might as well bag it.

DO YOU HAVE A SPIRIT TO SERVE?

Spirit. What a neat word. It's a word that connotes action, enthusiasm, energy, courage, liveliness, animation, drive, get-up and go, pep, vigor, vitality, character, passion and oomph. WOW! Organizations and leaders who exhibit spirit stand head and shoulders above others. They are positive and know that when times are tough, their spirit will pull them through. In addition to feeling good, their attitude is that much can be accomplished by developing a spirit to serve others.

It's All About Giving

The happiest people I know on this earth are those who serve others. They are genuinely concerned about the people they work with, and they take personal satisfaction out of seeing people progress. They feel the same about their families, friends and the community organizations to which they belong. They get "high" helping others and serve others because they want to and feel good about it.

Too Busy to Serve?

Many people say they are too busy to get involved in the community, and yet they spend a vast amount of time at work. These individuals feel important and indispensable. They feel like the company will self-destruct without them. They create a false sense of security within themselves and feel like they must be present at all times. They don't understand that one of the telltale signs of a great leader is not what happens when you're there, it's what happens when you're not there. And most of all, they can't comprehend that when they retire or leave the company, their inbox will always be full.

Opportunities Galore

If you sit back and think about it, there are so many opportunities where you can serve others. You might try reading to kids, serving meals to the homeless, working with organizations helping kids succeed, or taking time to share your experiences with others, either in a group or individual setting. You and your organization might want to get involved with the Make-A-Wish Foundation® or one of the many United Way agencies that are always in desperate need of volunteers. One thought is to get your family involved and to do a project together. It's a great lesson for your kids and one they will never forget.

When you grow up in a little town, as I did, everybody knows everybody. It is however a wonderful way to experience life. Like most towns, there were many wealthy people, many who had moderate incomes, and those who struggled. I can't ever remember a Thanksgiving going by that my dad and I didn't take dinner to someone in need. He always had a kind word for them and let them know he was concerned about their welfare. However, what I remember most of all was the look on their faces. That look has stuck with me all of these years and I still get the same euphoric feeling when I help others.

Just Do It

Take time to remember others. Do something nice for them and help their spirits soar. Inoculate them with a spirit that will help them through the trials and tribulations of life.

You see, a person with a spirit to serve does just that.

 Giraffism: When you give, you always get more in return.

I MADE A MISTAKE (BIG DEAL)

Have you ever worked for someone who delighted in catching people making mistakes? They act like big cats just waiting to pounce on their prey. They lie in wait, slithering around corners until someone does something wrong. What they don't understand is that they could make such a positive impact by catching people doing things right. These so-called "leaders" are control freaks whose actions demoralize others. They get their jollies by intimidating the people with whom they come in contact. They are truly the destroyers of a positive work environment.

No Pain, No Gain

Great (servant) leaders understand the value of people thinking for themselves and using their talents. They encourage their team-mates to try new and different approaches. They don't pounce on them when they make a mistake as they know that in an open, inno-vative environment, mistakes will occur. They always know that the only people who don't make mistakes are the people that don't do anything. And yes, you can have all of those people, as I want people who seek the new, and who regularly use their minds. They are the people who will take you to the next level.

Be Supportive

When people do make mistakes, as they will, don't hang them out to dry! Before making any assumptions, sit down and talk with them to find out what went wrong. Encourage them to be honest and to admit what went wrong. Let them know that trying to cover up mistakes gets cumbersome, difficult and stressful. We have great examples of leaders at the national, state and local levels who have tried to cover up things and, as we know, it always comes back to haunt them.

Get Over It

Once the person understands what the mistake resulted in, move on! Don't make World War III out of it. Most people feel bad that they let you down, and harping on it doesn't accomplish anything. Think of it this way. They didn't start off the morning saying, "I'm not going to do that right today." If they did, then you have the wrong teammates.

Don't Hammer People

Hammers are for nails, not for people. When you hit your finger with a hammer, it bruises it, turns yellow, green, black and ugly. Sometimes you lose the nail and it takes a long time for it to heal and grow back. The same principle holds true for people. Hammering them doesn't accomplish anything positive; in fact, it's the mistake you don't want to make or admit.

Don't Be a Copy Cat

Be different than the run-of-the-mill leader. Don't prove your superiority by making others feels bad. The greatest (servant) leaders on earth are like all of us in that they, too, make mistakes.

Talk with your people, let them know you care, catch them doing things right, encourage them, love them and let them know they make a difference. And when they do make a mistake, and they will, don't desert them. If you do, then you can simply say, "I made a mistake."

 Giraffism: The six most important words in the English language are "I admit that I was wrong," and they are the most difficult to say.

IF YOU THINK YOU'RE THE LONE RANGER, EVEN HE HAD TONTO!

Business is a team sport! And yet, many leaders try to "wing it" on their own thinking they can do it alone. Just think about some of the great sports teams in history—The Boston Celtics, the New York Yankees, the Pittsburgh Steelers, the San Francisco 49ers and the Los Angeles Lakers. True, they had a Bird, a Ruth, a Bradshaw, a Montana, and some "Magic," but it was the collective effort of all of the team members that made them successful. There are a lot of "superstars" in both sports and business, but unless they work with the team it's all for naught.

Work Together

Working together requires a lot of coordination and communication, and good leaders keep all members of the team informed. At Owens&Minor, once a product is sold it has to be picked, priced, invoiced, delivered and serviced. Each member of the team has a responsibility that they must carry out to ensure that the customer is totally and completely satisfied.

Recognize Others

One of the greatest things you can do as a leader is to recognize and thank other members of the team who were instrumental in some way. The sweetest words in the English language are a person's name on someone else's lips. We all like to be praised and thanked for a job well done. The thank you can come in the form of a telephone call, fax, note or face-to-face. Don't ever miss an opportunity to thank your teammates, as it is a source of energy for them.

Share with Others

Great leaders also share what has worked for them with other leaders in the organization. Selfish, self-centered leaders who don't share information with their teammates usually are only successful for a short period of time. Their star rises, but it falls quickly. Leaders who share with their teammates learn, grow and work together toward a common goal. The healthy competition that exists among them keeps them focused and sharp.

Be a Team

If you think about episodes of the Lone Ranger, you'll recall that Tonto was, in many cases, the eyes and ears for his sidekick. That's the same way it is in business. It's a great feeling when you have a team of people looking out for you.

I'm sure you've heard the catch phrase that there is "no I in Team." In my mind that is not true as each person brings their individual talents and dreams to the table. Some people bring more than others, but that's OK because what they bring becomes a part of what the team is all about.

The Lone Ranger and Tonto were a team and as they "cleaned up" the towns by exhibiting teamwork; you, too, can "clean up" and wipe away your competition.

Hi-Yo Silver...Away.

 Giraffism: Individuals don't win—teams do.

SECOND TO NONE

Every Sunday I have the privilege of attending Second Presbyterian Church (Second Pres) in Richmond, Virginia. Second Pres is a historic church located in the heart of the city. It has been making a difference in Richmond for 155 years by providing hospitality to the homeless, sheltering children, partnering with African-American churches, and ministering to its congregation.

Ben Sparks, the pastor at Second Pres, is a smart, wise and caring servant leader who takes pride in everything he does. And like most great servant leaders, he is a servant first and assumes leadership only if he sees it as the best way he can serve. Janet James, the associate pastor, is a great complement to Ben. Her mannerisms, body language and caring attitude, combined with her Tennessee accent, lets everyone know of her love for the human race and of her desire to be there for them.

Second Pres is truly second to none.

Think about it. Truly great people and great organizations are never satisfied with second best. They always strive to be the best at what they do. They work hard at improving every facet of what they do. They know that to consistently make a difference they must be at the top of their game.

Who's Playing for Second?

A few years ago, Larry Bird, the great Hall of Fame basketball player from the Boston Celtics, was getting ready to compete in the NBA three-point shooting contest. When asked how he thought he'd do he simply replied, "Who's playing for second?"

Being the best at what you do is an attitude. If you approach every situation feeling that you'll accomplish your goal, chances are good that you will. That's why you see sports teams who are not as talented as others upset their opponent. They believe they can do it...and they do.

Take a Second "Look"

One of the things we all need to do is take a second and learn from others. One of the best organizations at what they do is the highly respected Southeastern Institute of Research in Richmond, Virginia. For years they have been called upon by state and national government, educational institutions and businesses throughout the east coast to conduct surveys and research.

What makes them so good and why do their clients continually go back and go back again?

One has to look no further than SIR's leadership. Co-owners Richard Steele and Bob Miller are true professionals who look after their employees. They believe in them and give them the latitude to do their jobs. They understand that the way they treat their employees is the way their employees will treat their customers. And they have the customers to prove it.

Call SIR's switchboard and talk with Eulah. You'll discover someone whose smile comes right through the phone and who is truly a "Director of First Impressions." Talk with Linda Walton or Linda Singleton-Driscoll, and you'll discover two employees who take pride in and care about not only what they do but about you. That attitude permeates the walls at SIR and is infectious to everyone involved. They are the reasons why Southeastern Institute of Research is second to none.

The Seconds Are Ticking Away

The 21st century, like other centuries, will be a time of change. And those individuals who have made a commitment to being second to none will stand head and shoulders above the crowd. Take time now to determine what you need to do to be at the top of your class.

Don't put off until tomorrow what you can accomplish today. Be proactive, take the bull by the horns and get on with it now. Don't settle for second, third or fourth. If you do, you'll wind up having "second thoughts" that "if I'd only done that I'd…." Make it your personal goal to be second to none.

 Giraffism: Nobody remembers who finished second.

I Gave at the Office

If you talk with successful people and ask them about the keys to their success, they'll almost always tell you about a person or mentor who was instrumental in their lives. This mentor served as a friend, confidant, coach, counselor, cheerleader and someone who was always there for advice or assistance.

Webster defines a mentor as "an experienced and trusted advisor." And while this is certainly true, it is really much more than that. The best mentors I've known are passionate about life, about people and about their work. They truly love what they do and do what they love. They are what I call "servant leaders" because they experience a real high in serving others and making a difference.

What do servant leaders give as presents all throughout the year? Here are some of the ways you can be a mentor to co-workers and employees.

The Gift of Time

Time is a precious commodity. We are all busy in both our personal and professional lives. Thus, one of the greatest things you do for people is take the time to let them know you care, that you're interested in them, and that you're there to talk with them.

Most of us have a tendency to "jump into" the conversation before we should. Good mentors are patient, understanding listeners who don't waste energy "talking."

The Gift of Energy

Another gift you can give is to help energize others. There are times when we all need a boost or need our batteries recharged. Great mentors sense when people are downtrodden and provide the spark to help see them through whatever the problem may be. That spark could be a few words of wisdom, a pat on the back or a reassuring comment.

People are persuaded by reason, but moved by emotion. That's why it's such a great feeling to be around upbeat, positive people. We have a tendency to listen to them, to be more open with them, to share and to have fun. Think about the teachers or speakers that you've heard. You listen to and respect the ones who are excited about their message and who are expressive and passionate.

The Gift of "Walking the Talk"

Perhaps the best gift you can give others is to follow your own advice. It's one thing to give advice to others, but it only has true meaning when you "walk the talk." Like children, we learn from watching and observing others and actions certainly speak louder than words.

I think the following poem by Edgar Guest sums it up best:

I'd rather see a sermon than hear one any day.
I'd rather one would walk with me than merely point the way.
For the eye is a better pupil and more willing than the ear.
Fine counsel is confusing but example is always clear.
And the best of all the preachers are the ones that live their creed,
For to see the good in action is what everybody needs.
I can soon learn how to do it if you let me see it done.
I can watch your hands in action, but your tongue too fast may run.
And the lectures you deliver may be very wise and true,
But I'd rather get my lessons from observing what you do.
For I may misunderstand the high advice you give.
There is no misunderstanding how you act and how you live.

Make a resolution to give your time, energy and enthusiasm to others as a mentor. When you give, you always get more in return.

 Giraffism: Be an inspiration to others and "give" to them.

SOLID AS A ROCK

We sometimes hear the phrase that an individual or organization is as "solid as a rock." That phrase conjures up images in our mind of something that is durable, strong, solid and impenetrable.

One of my good friends is Charlie Luck, IV, President of Luck Stone. Luck Stone has been in business for over 75 years and, like the product they sell, they are a solid organization.

How does a company like Luck Stone go about becoming solid as a rock? Are there any big secrets? The answer is there is no big secret and no magic involved. It is a matter of paying attention to the basics that propel businesses to the top. It is establishing a process and making sure that it is continually updated and improved.

Orientation Is Key

First and foremost, when a new worker walks in the door on day one, it is critical that you ensure he/she understands everything about your company. This includes your company's history; the amount of business you do; who your customers are; the products or services you sell; your competition; and your overall quality and service process. The more your teammates know, the better they will feel about themselves and the company.

When you take the time to orient your workers, they feel they are working for a caring company and that you are interested in their careers and want them to succeed. Even tell them about simple things that you take for granted, like where to locate the copy and fax machines, where workers go on break, where to get office supplies, and how to use the telephone.

At Owens&Minor we provide every new teammate with an orientation notebook entitled, "Almost Everything You Need to Know." Updating the notebook is a continuous process because we want our teammates to have the most up-to-date information.

Hand-in-hand with orientating your teammates is maintaining consistent communication with them. A well-informed teammate is a productive teammate, but companies often struggle because of communication issues.

At Owens&Minor we have many communication vehicles. There are the standard means like e-mail, fax and voice mail. In addition to our electronic bulletin board, we use old-fashioned bulletin boards that have headings such as "Newsmaker," "Team Talk" and "On the Wire." Bulletin boards are located in each of our distribution centers manned by coordinators who regularly post and remove information. We also use our internal publication, "The Distributor," to convey information.

Finally, we post messages on our welcome sign at the entrance of our building and memos in our elevators. You really can't over-communicate good information to your teammates.

In an earlier chapter, I referred to an Earle Nightingale quote that, "The effectiveness of one's life is determined by the effectiveness of one's communicative skills." Just think about it. Friendships end, deals fall through, people get lost and divorce occurs because of a lack of communication. Taking the time to communicate is well worth the effort and will pay off in dividends for you and your organization.

Knowledge Is Power

If your company is to succeed, you must have knowledgeable teammates. You are only as strong as your weakest link, so it's impor-tant that you provide the necessary training to ensure that your team-mates know what to do.

One of the reasons people fail on the job is that they don't know how to do it. Take the time to work with your people and teach them the tricks of the trade. Be a coach, teacher and mentor, as there is nothing more rewarding than watching people develop and mature.

While you should be there for them and guide them, you should also entrust your workers by making them accountable and letting them own problems. You'll be amazed how much they grow and how responsible they become.

An Ounce of Recognition Is Worth a Pound of Control

Lastly, take the time to recognize your teammates for jobs well done. We all get so busy and so wrapped up in our everyday activities that we forget to applaud, laud and thank our employees for their good work.

A recent survey conducted by Deloitte & Touche indicated that of the 12 things that employees cite as their top motivators, the number one need by far is "the feeling like I've done a good job." We all like to be recognized, and when we are, we perform at high levels.

There are many ways to recognize individuals that don't cost an arm and a leg. It could be a phone call, a letter, a plaque, a pen or some memento that makes reference to a job they have done well. Remember, the cost of recognizing someone is far less than the cost of not doing so.

Recognition, orientation, communication and knowledge are the necessary ingredients to form your ROCK. Make sure you focus on each of these ingredients and continually improve them.

 Giraffism: Organizations, like rocks, need to be solid in their practices and beliefs.

IS YOUR NAME CLARK KENT?
He knows all about change

Faster than a speeding bullet, more powerful than a locomotive, able to leap tall buildings in a single bound. It's a bird, it's a plane and, as we all know, it's Superman.

If you think about it, the Clark Kent/Superman personality is all about change. It's about a mild-mannered reporter, lacking confidence and self-worth, who changes into a super human being who believes anything is possible. Life is all about change, adapting to different situations and meeting the demands of the future. The most successful people I know are those who can change and/or adapt to change.

But change is scary, difficult and not easy for most of us. How do you go about instituting change at work, home, your church or in the community where people don't get frustrated, feel threatened and get their feathers ruffled?

Prepare for Change

First and foremost, we must prepare people for change. Just telling someone to do something is not reason enough. Point out existing problems and why change would be beneficial to everyone involved.

It could be simple as changing the time that your children go to bed. Let them know the reasons why and how they will benefit from getting an extra hour of sleep. Or, it could be changing the time your team comes to work. Again, let them know the benefits and what's in it for them.

"We've Always Done It That Way"

In his best selling book, *Teaching the Elephant to Dance,* Jim Belasco talks about American business being shackled by the chains of conditioning and habit. I have a saying that "If you live with what you're successful with today, you'll die with it tomorrow." Yet, many businesses are slow to change and that spells disaster for them. They get very complacent at what they do and feel that their way of doing business will last forever.

A great example of this would be Ben Franklin store's lack of interest in franchising Sam Walton's discount stores in small towns. They felt the concept just wouldn't work. Not a good decision. Wal*Mart only did $193 billion in 2000! Not bad for a concept that was not, shall we say, mainstream.

Leaders Make the Difference

Why does one organization thrive and another hang on for dear life? The difference lies in the leadership of the organization. Great leaders understand the value of change and what it can mean to the company and its employees.

For leaders, success is the enemy and staying on top is much harder than getting there. Leaders understand they need the talents of their teammates and must entrust employees to use their own creativity, skills and expertise to make change happen. Leaders also know that their people must have input as to what change should look like and must be kept informed to the nth degree.

In their best selling book, *The Leadership Challenge*, Jim Kouzes and Barry Posner point out that the most admired leaders are those who are forward-looking. People are willing to follow leaders who have a dream and a vision and who dare to be different.

Teamwork Will Get You There

To change, you must create an environment where people truly enjoy working together. Employees must be open, honest, enthusiastic and possess a "we'll get it done" attitude. There is no room for the faint of heart.

Clark Kent and Superman are visibly different, but inside they both have that burning desire to change things and make them right. Their separate identities point out that you don't have to be a Superman to change things, just the desire and intestinal fortitude to do so.

 Giraffism: The most successful people I know are those who can change, adapt to change, and prepare others for change.

IF IT'S ON FIRE...PUT IT OUT

Meet Jack McElfish, the City of Richmond's Fire Chief/Director of Emergency Services and you'll realize instantly that he's a pro at what he does. Gary Briese, Executive Director, International Association of Fire Chiefs, states it best: "Chief McElfish is considered a national leader, an innovator, an opinion setter. He is recognized as one of the most progressive leaders in fire service and has a reputation for being plain spoken, honest, forthright and creative."

He's a team player who is not afraid to get involved and make decisions. Most of all, he has fun at what he does.

Think about it. Whether it's at work, home, church, Little League, Junior League, Boy Scouts, or any activity where you're involved, "fires" or burning issues erupt. And once the issue erupts, unless you immediately address it, it sizzles, gains momentum and spreads like wildfire. To make matters worse, there are people who love to "fan" the fires and watch them burn.

Don't Procrastinate

When something like this takes place, it is so key to take action and not let it simmer. One of my favorite quotes is from Dante's

Inferno, and it simply states that "The hottest places in hell are reserved for those individuals who in times of moral crisis maintain their neutrality."

When you experience a problem, address it head on. Take time to listen to all the facts, hear everyone out, and then make a decision. Most of us dislike being around those who procrastinate. They cause us frustration and at times make us downright angry. There's nothing worse than dealing with someone who states, "I believe strongly both ways."

Shift Out of "Neutral"

When people are neutral on issues, nothing happens. It's like putting your car in neutral. All one does is rev the motor, "rock" back and forth and waste energy. Don't be afraid to take a stand and make a decision. People like to be associated with people who are doers and decision-makers. Doers and decision-makers emit a feeling of confidence and make those around them feel good.

Don't Hesitate…Do It

If Chief McElfish just watched things happen, the city would be in serious trouble. He knows that when he receives an emergency call his team must be decisive and prepared to act. In medical emergencies, like business, time is of the essence, so the chief must have his people prepared. When the time comes to act, they do, and do so in a confident and effective manner. They know how to put out the fires and take care of problems.

Attitude, Desire, Passion

So much of what I'm talking about is attitude, desire and passion. General Thomas Jonathan "Stonewall" Jackson once stated, "You may be whatever you resolve to be." And that is so true. We all have within us the power and the ability to excel, to do good and great things, and to make a difference. Unfortunately, some of us never unharness or unleash our potential, and it remains idle and untapped. And as my friend Chief McElfish so eloquently states, "It's a fire without a spark."

Working Together Is Key

In putting out fires, it's important to share thoughts and work together. Everyone brings something to the table and all of those special talents are needed to address the issue at hand. There's a fire burning in most all of us, and it's important that we put it "out" on the table. The top organizations and leaders in America are great at locating burning issues and working together to solve them.

Chief McElfish knows all the modern techniques for extinguishing fires, but bottom line for him and for all of us is to simply…put them out.

 *Giraffism: **Don't be a wuss…make decisions.***

WHO ARE YOUR HEROES?

Heroes come in all shapes and sizes. They are people who give unselfishly of themselves. They are not limited to any one profession. They are committed to making a difference in the lives of others and when called upon, they do. One has to look no further than the events of September 11, 2001, to get a feel for what heroism is all about.

Organizational Heroes

Have you ever thought about the heroes in your organization and their value? They are the people who go the extra mile to ensure that customers' needs are satisfied. They are always there to help others, whether they are fellow teammates on the job or non-profit organizations in the community.

Heroes are people who don't know the meaning of the phrase, "It's not my job." They always have a smile on their face because they believe no task is insurmountable. They are the teammates who truly are "heroes."

Unsung Heroes

A great speaker and writer I once heard tells the story of a visit he made to see renowned heart surgeon Michael DeBakey at Houston's Methodist Hospital. The only time Dr. DeBakey would see him was at 5:30 in the morning prior to his first surgery.

As he was walking down the hall he stopped to talk with a gentleman who was singing and mopping the corridor to the operating room. He asked the attendant why he was so happy. His answer was a classic: "Me and the Doc are saving lives!"

Heroes come in all shapes and sizes. I have long felt that everyone brings something to the table. Some bring more than others, but what counts is how you interact with people.

The attendant he met truly felt that he made a difference…and he did! He saw the big picture and realized his job was essential in ensuring that there was a sterile environment. He took pride in his work because he felt like he was an integral part of the team.

Your company should also recognize its heroes. Drop them a note, leave them a voice-mail message, encourage them, thank them and reward them. They are the people who separate you from your competitors. Their actions make lasting impressions.

Cultivate a Stable of Heroes

How do you go about identifying your heroes? Fortunately, it's not hard to do. The hard part is developing a team of heroes where everyone feels that they make a difference and contribute.

I am sometimes asked how many customer service representatives we employ at Owens&Minor. I rapidly reply "3,000." When I'm asked how many teammates we employ, my reply is the same! Every teammate is a customer service representative and we want them all to be heroes.

I've always felt that heroes need to be at the forefront, interacting with external customers to perpetuate a positive corporate image. Therefore, if I had to pick one position to place a hero, it would be at the reception desk.

The receptionist gives people the first impression they have of your company, whether it's via phone or in person. First impressions are lasting impressions, so it is important to make the first one count.

Cultivate and identify the heroes in your organization. Their heroic acts will make you a hero in the eyes of your customers.

 Giraffism: Heroes are special people.

You'll travel an uncluttered road!

GO THE EXTRA MILE

There is no doubt that individuals and organizations that go the extra mile for their customers travel on uncrowded roads. Everybody and his brother talk about providing superior customer service, but in reality only about 20% really do. Going the extra mile takes a lot of effort, commitment, and love for the business and your customers.

At Owens&Minor we work with over 1,200 vendors. And even though we are buying from them, we consider them our customers. We sit on the same side of the table with them and treat them as partners as opposed to adversaries. We know that by sharing and working with them, we'll both succeed.

One of our best partners at supplying our needs is Adco Associates. Adco supplies us with our sweatshirts, t-shirts, pens, pencils, towels, cups, caps, personalized stickee-notes, and you name it. The CEO of Adco is Sondra Mitchell-Bennett, and we have had a working relationship for the past 15 years.

What makes Adco and Sondra Mitchell-Bennett stand out? Why do we continue buying from them? What do they do differently?

For starters, they are always there when you need them. Calls are returned promptly and efficiently. When you talk with Sondra you know she cares about you and your business. She makes you feel like you're the only customer she has (and she has many). Most of all, she lets you know that she appreciates the business you are giving her company and that she will always go the extra mile to exceed your expectations. In 14 years of doing business with Adco and Sondra Mitchell, I've yet to be disappointed.

Lots of Smileage

I recently had the privilege of meeting and talking with the East Coast Oil Company leadership team. East Coast, "Where your Mom would stop," is committed to taking care of their customers and providing superior customer service. One of the signs they proudly display talks about the "smileage" you receive at East Coast. And they live up to this!

That's so important because one of the cardinal rules of customer service is to smile at your customers.

When you smile at people, it lets them know that you care and that you're interested in them. And smiling doesn't only pertain to the look on one's face. Practice what I call PASIYV (Put A Smile In Your Voice). Be professional, responsive and expressive. It makes all the difference in the world.

Take the High Road

So much of going the extra mile pertains to one's attitude. There's no doubt that one's attitude will determine their altitude and what they can attain in life. When you take the high road, the distance is shorter between two points. You get there quicker and time flies. You feel good about yourself and it shows. On the high road you see things differently and others look up to you. It's what I call a "high five" experience.

Miles Ahead

Going the extra mile puts you miles ahead of others. The truly great organizations and leaders in the U.S. out-distance their competitors in so many ways. They know that to stay at the top they must continually raise the bar in all areas. They understand that it's difficult to get to the top, but that it's more difficult to stay there.

One of the ways they maintain their leadership is by constantly creating the new. In order to do this, they out-think and out-perform their competition. This gives them the edge and allows them to move forward in a confident manner. They never have to look back, as they are prepared for the road ahead.

Make it a habit to go the extra mile at work, at home and at play. If you do, you'll own the road and reach your destination far ahead of others. In fact, you'll be so far ahead they'll run out of gas trying to catch you.

 Giraffism: Companies and individuals who go the extra mile are a mile ahead.

HOW HIGH CAN YOU CLIMB?
Attitude + Aptitude = Altitude

Rising high into the sky! Soaring with the best. Distinguishing yourself from your competition. Creating customer successes.

That's what an effective Customer Service Process can mean for your company. And yet, despite the numerous books that have been written on the subject and the many dollars paid consultants for quality advice, few companies have achieved success.

Why is this the case? What is the mystery? Who holds the key? The answer in my mind is simple: leadership and attitude. World-class leaders set the stage for quality programs through their positive attitude and dedication to great performance.

They realize that teammates are persuaded by reason, but moved by emotion. Great leaders work for their teammates, always keeping them informed, making them feel good about themselves and preparing them for change.

Most of all, great leaders let their teammates know that they make a difference, that they are needed, and that their opinions and ideas are valued.

It's All About PMA

Having a positive mental attitude and applying one's skills are a tough combination to beat. So many people go through life saying, "I won't be able to do that." And, guess what? Those people don't accomplish anything.

I love to play tennis and I do so as often as I can. I always tell people that I've never lost a match in my life…I just ran out of time!

The individuals who best serve their customers are positive and inspirational. They don't know the word "no." They don't offer excuses when a customer calls with a problem. Rather, their standard answer is, "I apologize for the inconvenience. What can we do to make it right?"

These people turn negatives into positives. They make mountains into molehills. They look at problems as opportunities and use their knowledge and skills to help others achieve success. Most of all, they know they cannot lose as long as their customer wins.

Isn't it great to talk with someone who has a positive attitude? No one likes to work with people who complain, who offer excuses and who are flat out negative.

PMA People Win

People with positive attitudes are winners because they are determined, set goals and concentrate on tasks at hand. They don't let the "little things" alter their course, and they know there is no future in saying, "It can't be done."

Positive people work hard at applying themselves. They take risks. They seek the new and make things happen. Sure, they will have occasional setbacks. Yet, those with a positive attitude will win more than they will lose.

A few years ago, a book entitled *The Sky's the Limit* by Dr. Wayne Dwyer, was a national best seller. This book is based on the premise that with a positive attitude, you can control your own destiny and reach plateaus heretofore not in sight.

That premise comes true when you apply your knowledge and skills and possess a winning attitude that is infectious.

 Giraffism: Life is 90% attitude and 10% aptitude.

ARE YOU RAISING THE BAR...EVERY DAY?

At the 1996 Summer Olympics in Atlanta, I had the privilege of watching the greatest high jumpers in the world. Inch by inch, they raised the bar to a new level. If they failed on the first try, they prepared themselves mentally and physically to try once again to soar to new heights. When they conquered the stated height, they celebrated their accomplishment.

As I watched them prepare for this event, they all exhibited similar characteristics. First and foremost, it was obvious that they were focused. Each participant would walk up to the bar, study it and mentally measure it. I imagine they were visually clearing the bar in much the same way that successful speakers visualize how audiences will react to their successful presentation.

After studying the bar, they returned to their starting positions. At this point, I used binoculars to view their faces. As you would imagine, there were looks of determination, calmness, fear, anxiety, intensity—you name it.

If you think about it, there is a great analogy to what I've just described when it comes to you or your organization's ability to get better every day. Those companies and individuals who excel at this are those who look to the future and expect to gradually raise the bar so that they reach a new level which distinguishes them from their competition.

So, how do you go about doing this? What do you need to do to be the best of the best?

One at a Time

I sometimes get calls from individuals who are responsible for their company's quality/customer service program. Many are frustrated with what is taking place, as their progress is somewhat stymied.

As I listen and talk with them, I soon discover that one of their problems is that they are trying to "eat" the whole cake as opposed to one slice at a time. Don't do it! Identify one weakness, focus on it and dedicate the necessary resources to make it better. Remember, it makes a greater impact to improve one area 100% as opposed to improving 100 areas 1%.

Perfect Practice Makes Perfect

One of the reasons individuals fail is that they don't know how to do what is expected. Make sure your team understands what it takes to get the job done. Give them the necessary training to help them succeed and put it into practice. Some companies and individuals don't provide knock-your-socks-off service because they don't know how to excel. Again, it's like the high jumper who doesn't understand the techniques necessary to make a successful jump.

Once you have the techniques, practice, practice, practice them. It's not practice that makes perfect. It's perfect practice that makes perfect. And remember, you'll probably fail many times until you get it right. The only people who don't fail are those who don't do anything, who play it safe and who have no initiative and desire to raise their bar. They would much rather watch things happen as opposed to making them happen.

Go for It!

There's an old adage that says he who hesitates is lost. If the high jumper hesitates, he or she is in serious trouble. That split second of indecision is a big factor in whether the jump is successful or not. Make a decision and go for it. Your attitude will determine so much of your success.

Make it a goal to raise your bar…every day. Like the high jumper, make sure you measure your progress, because that will be a gauge as to how you are doing. You see, being the best is an everyday job…every day.

 Giraffism: If you raise the bar every day, you and your organization will reach new heights.

LOOKING FOR A LEADER…HIRE A CARPENTER

Like the flu vaccine in 2000, there is a national shortage of good leaders. Companies, churches, educational institutions, hospitals and community organizations are constantly on the lookout for leaders who can lead others and take them to the Promised Land. Leading others sounds easy, but it takes a special person to get others to realize their potential and achieve new heights.

Thousands of books and articles have been written on leadership, and we are constantly bombarded with literature, mailings and TV advertisements on leadership seminars and workshops. They all offer good and different thoughts on what it takes to be a good leader. There is, however, no magic to leadership. It's all about building, dreaming, creating and making a difference. It's really all about being a carpenter.

Have Vision

Think about it. Carpenters have a lot of vision. They start a project with various materials and mold them into something that takes shape and form. They start by creating a solid foundation and build from the ground up. Along the way they rely on their vision, making whatever modifications necessary to ensure that the structure is functional and sound. Great leaders do the same in shaping the people they mentor.

Use the Right Tools

Carpenters know exactly what tools are necessary to complete a project. They know that if the job calls for a hacksaw, a wood saw won't get it done. They know what size nails to use on a job in order for the structure to remain intact. They know that if they misplace the nail or put it too close to the end or side of a board, the board will split. The same holds true for leaders. They know if they select the right tools and courses of action for a person, the person will gain confidence and not be fragmented. Like carpenters, they understand that one size does not fit all and that they must select the appropriate tool to complete their project. Use of the wrong tool won't get the job done.

Hammers Are for Nails

Carpenters understand that hammers are for nails and not for people. They know the trauma one experiences when they hit their finger with a hammer and the bruise it leaves. It takes a while for the finger to heal, and sometimes it doesn't function as well. The same holds true for great leaders. They too understand that hammers are for nails and not for people. They treat their people fairly and with respect. Like the carpenter, when the nail is not going straight, they take corrective action and do so in a forthright and positive manner.

Measure Twice, Cut Once

Great carpenters measure twice and cut once. They are very action-oriented and not of the fire-ready-aim school. If so, they would waste a lot of lumber and materials. Again, the same holds true for great leaders. They are not afraid to make decisions. They aren't neutral on anything and are willing to take a risk. Before doing so, however, they look and weigh all of the options.

Be a Builder

Great carpenters and leaders are builders. Sometimes to build, they have to tear down what was there. They know that some foundations are weak and to complete the end product they must start over. Whether you're building from the ground up or renovating an existing structure, the construction remains the same.

A carpenter? If my writing isn't convincing enough, think of the greatest carpenter and builder of men…one born in a village near Jerusalem called Bethlehem. And all I can add to that is, Amen.

 Giraffism: Great leaders, like great carpenters, possess all of the tools they need to build a structure.

WHERE HAVE YOU GONE— AMY, LETITIA AND EMILY?

In my mind, the two most important words in the English language—or any language for that matter— are "thank you." For years, Emily Post, Amy Vanderbilt and Letitia Baldridge have pointed out the proper way to address people who have given us gifts or gone out of their way to support us.

Survey after survey points out the need to be recognized, the need to feel like we've made a difference. Remember how it was when you were a child and someone complimented or recognized you? It was a great feeling that we treasured.

Yet somewhere in our maturation process from child to adult, we've forgotten the words that brought smiles to our faces. Saying "thank you" is becoming scarcer than hen's teeth.

Measure It

Warren Bennis, renowned author of many books on leadership, conducted a survey of 10,000 employees. The survey presented 10 characteristics relative to job satisfaction and asked the employees to rank them on a scale of one to 10, one being the most important.

After receiving the results of this survey, Bennis talked with the managers and supervisors of these employees and asked them how they thought their employees ranked the 10 characteristics.

A Little Note Will Do…

It wasn't surprising to me that number two on the employees' list was being shown appreciation for their work. When your teammates do something special or go beyond the call of duty, take the time to write them a note. Typed notes are okay, but there is nothing more personal than penning a note of thanks.

When you do write the note, write the way you talk. Too many people try to use big, sophisticated words that even they don't understand. Instead of trying to say, "I am extremely exhilarated by the manner in which you satisfy our business partner," simply say, "You sure know how to take care of our customers." Any note you write should utilize the KISS method (Keep It Simple and Sincere) and be limited to one page.

…Or a Phone Call

Another way to thank or compliment teammates is to pick up Alexander Graham Bell's invention and tell them what you feel. If you can't reach them personally, leave a voice mail letting them know that you called. It is a nice feeling to check one's voice mail and hear a pleasant, complimentary message.

But That's Your Job

When I talk with organizations around the country, some team leaders fail to recognize their teammates because "it's their job to carry out their responsibilities in an exceptional manner." That is true...but when people know you appreciate what they do, they will move mountains for you.

Think of the cost of recognizing teammates as opposed to the cost of not recognizing them. A simple "Thank you" or "You did a great job" or "Keep up the good work" goes a long way and costs nothing, other than the time it takes you to utter these words.

Let your teammates know the criteria for awards and make sure all of your leaders are involved. Present awards at meetings or other company gatherings. Nothing makes teammates feel better than receiving recognition in front of their peers. Again, the cost of setting up a recognition process is minimal compared to the cost of not doing it.

Make Emily, Amy and Letitia proud by taking the time to recognize others. It's a small price to pay for such huge dividends.

 Giraffism: A little thanks goes a long way.

ARE YOU AN ANNUAL, A PERENNIAL, OR A WEED?

If you're a music fan you probably remember the hit song entitled, "Where Have All the Flowers Gone?" And when you think of flowers, annuals and perennials come to mind. Annuals live only for a year or less, while perennials span a period of time. The same thing happens with leaders, although lately we seem to have a shortage of perennial leaders.

Our recent leaders have been more of the annual or semi-annual type; and in many cases, we find a few weeds that have taken over. Over the years, we've been blessed with great leaders...leaders in church, state, business and the community.

Leaders who were smart, knowledgeable and imaginative. Leaders who were passionate about their cause, who were sensitive to the needs of others and who truly cared.

Be a Giver

Winston Churchill was one of those great leaders. He could inspire a nation with a few meaningful words. Likewise, he could deliver long oratories and mesmerize his audience.

Like most great leaders, Churchill was a giver. He once said, "We make a living by what we get, but we make a life by what we give." He truly believed this and gave of his time and talents to teach others the price of greatness.

Great leaders possess positive attitudes and inspire others to reach new heights. They help ordinary people achieve extraordinary things. They are living proof of the message when you believe you can, you can.

Great leaders evoke change and live their dreams. Change for the sake of change is absolutely worthless, but change with a purpose in mind and to make things better is essential. Nobody epitomizes this more than Martin Luther King, Jr.

Show Passion

Martin Luther King, Jr. had a passion for equality for all. That passion was evident to everyone he touched. When you have the kind of passion he exhibited, change occurs. There's nothing stronger than having a passion for a person or a cause.

Dreaming is a huge part of leadership, as dreamers have a vision for the future. Dr. King dreamed and soared to great heights. He refused to take no for an answer and lived his dream.

Be an Achiever

Maggie Lena Mitchell Walker was a very special woman and a great leader. Richmond, Virginia was Maggie Walker's birthplace, and she loved the city so much she spent her entire life there. From her humble beginnings (her mother had been a slave) she grew up to become the first woman bank director in America.

Her bank, founded as The Saint Luke's Penny Savings Bank, absorbed Richmond's other African-American banks under the name of The Consolidated Bank and Trust Company. She has long been recognized as one of the nation's most successful entrepreneurs. What made Maggie Walker so special? Why was she recognized as a great leader? Like other great leaders, she too had a vision. She encouraged her race to get more education and better jobs.

She was a very gifted speaker who could move her audience. She was very religious and stressed the commandment, "Love thy neighbor as thyself." What more could you ask for in a leader.

Be a Student of History

Vision, passion, determination, commitment, a caring attitude, and a common sense approach are what leadership is all about.

Gil Minor III, Chairman and Chief Executive Officer of Owens&Minor, always states that history is a record of the past and a blueprint for the future.

Let's learn from past leaders, build upon their strengths, improve upon their weaknesses and blossom into effective, caring leaders.

 Giraffism: Everybody follows and learns from a good leader.

YOU GOTTA HAVE HEART

Years ago, there was a popular song that started, "You gotta have heart, miles and miles of heart." What reminded me of this song is a customer service seminar I did recently with Jacqueline Ukrop of Ukrop's Super Markets.

Jacqueline is a bright, vivacious young lady with a spontaneous, unbridled enthusiasm. Like her father Bobby and Uncle Jim, she has an uncanny ability to understand who her customers are and what needs to be done to take care of their needs. Jacqueline thrives on working with and helping others.

One of the things Jacqueline brought to our seminar was heart. She has a heart of gold that is as competitive as the heart of a lion. As we discussed the word "heart" and how important it is, Jacqueline unfolded an acronym that should be mandatory for everyone's customer service mantra—manual or program.

H...ear

If you really care about your customers, always take the time to listen to what they have to say. The greatest salespeople I know have never been the best talkers, but they are the best listeners. When you really listen, you get a true understanding of what the other person is experiencing or has experienced.

The best customer service organizations I know are those where team leaders listen to their teammates about how to better serve their customers. Remember that the person closest to the customer is best suited to know what the customer needs and wants.

E...mpathize

Let your customers know you have a heart and, more importantly, you have their best interests at heart. When a problem occurs, there's nothing wrong with saying, "I understand how you feel, because if I were in your situation I'd feel the same way."

We all make mistakes and fail at times and there's nothing wrong with admitting that we blew it. When you are honest with people, their respect for you grows.

A...pologize

Once you admit a mistake, follow with a sincere apology. Apologize for the organization, your teammates and for you. Let customers know that the service they received from you is not standard for the company and that your company is committed to excellence.

Again, be open and honest in your apology.

R...espond

Now that you've apologized, the most important thing is to take action. Let the customer know that you will personally ensure that the situation is corrected in a prompt, efficient manner.

Utilize the word "we" as much as possible to let your customer know that an entire organization is behind your actions. For example, you could say, "We will make sure to correct the problem, and I personally will make sure it happens."

T...hank

Last, but certainly not least, thank customers for their business, patience and understanding. Let them know how much you value them and their business. Once more, assure them that your organization will continue to work hard every day to earn their patronage.

If you take this information to heart, you will capture the heart and soul of your customers.

 Giraffism: You have to love your customers.

IT'S A BIRD…IT'S A PLANE… WAIT…IT'S A CUSTOMER

With all of the emphasis and hullabaloo on customer service during the past ten years it's amazing how few organizations really understand and practice customer service. It's true that many companies have slogans emphasizing customer service. These slogans focus on the fact that the customer is king and that the customer signs their paychecks. Unfortunately, most of these words are just that…WORDS.

The organizations that provide superior service practice what they preach. They understand that the leadership of the company must be totally committed to customer service and must support it at every level. They also understand who their customers are and the importance of keeping the lines of communication open at all times. Most of all, they have a structure in place that epitomizes servant leadership.

Who Are Your Customers?

Customers come in all shapes and sizes. Someone recently asked me who our customers are at Owens&Minor and I simply replied, "Everyone with whom we come in contact." When you treat everyone you meet like they are a customer, it lets them know you care. It lets them know that you're interested in them and they are special. All of the great customer service companies practice this philosophy and that is why they are so successful.

What Do They Want?

People always ask me, "How does Owens&Minor define customer service?" My answer is always the same; "We don't, our customers do!" Don't try to guess what your customers want—ask them. Great companies are extremely proactive and are continually taking the pulse of their customers. They routinely ask their customers, "What are we doing right? What are we doing wrong? What can we do to serve your needs better?" Customers love companies that take an interest in them and that listen to and act on their suggestions.

How Can You Raise the Bar?

The best way to raise the bar and create world-class customer service is to ensure that your internal customer service is second to none. The best and most profitable customer service companies I know are those who understand that their teammates come first. The way you treat your teammates is the way they treat your customers. Ukrop's, Nordstrom, Southwest Airlines, Home Depot, Scott&Stringfellow,

Disney, and the Chesterfield County, Virginia, Fire Department are great examples of putting this principle into practice.

Take Pride in Everything You Do

The word PRIDE has a wonderful ring to it. It connotes excellence, determination and…

If you use the word PRIDE as an acronym as we do at Owens&Minor, the 'P' stands for Professionalism. It is key that we be professional in dealing with our teammates and customers. The 'R' stands for Responsiveness. Response time should be measured in minutes, not hours, as people judge us by how quickly we follow through. The letter 'I' stands for Integrity and Honor and is indeed self-explanatory. The 'D' is for Delighting customers and making them smile. And the 'E' is for Exceeding Expectations. Customers expect you to meet their expectations. Great companies go the extra mile and exceed them.

If you want to soar like a bird or a plane you don't have to be Superman. You simply need to take care of your customers. If you do, they will take care of you and your business will grow by "leaps and bounds."

 Giraffism: You don't have to be Superman to provide super service.

A MINOR GIRAFFE THAT MAKES A MAJOR DIFFERENCE

Owens&Minor is a Fortune 500 company and the nation's largest supplier of branded medical/surgical supplies. It has been in business for 120 years and has shown phenomenal growth. It is truly a growth company and the numbers speak for themselves. The company grew from $7 million dollars in '59, to $20 million in '69, to $100 million in '79, to $1 billion in '89, and to $3.2 billion in '99.

The driving force behind Owens&Minor and its unique culture is G. Gilmer Minor, III. He is the fourth generation of Minors to run Owens&Minor. What makes him so successful, and why does he have the admiration and respect of all of his peers and teammates?

The answer is simple. Gil Minor not only has integrity, but he walks the talk. His actions and intentions are never in conflict with each other. He has character that shines through like a beacon of light. And like most great leaders, this character intensifies in critical and pressurized situations. When the pressure is on, that's when he is the coolest.

Meetings of the Minds

Gil Minor understands the value of recognizing others. He understands that the number one need of Americans is the need to be recognized. With this thought in mind, he pays yearly visits to as many of Owens&Minor's distribution centers as he possibly can. When the company was smaller he could visit all of them. Now he gets to one-third to one-half of them in a given year.

When Gil Minor visits these centers, he makes it a practice to talk with every teammate. He asks them about their families, their hobbies and their work. He asks what they like best about working at Owens&Minor, what they like least, and what the company can do to help them be successful. He then takes this information and feeds it back to his leadership team. Gil understands the value of feedback from his teammates, but more importantly, following through on their requests.

Open Door

If you visit the third floor of Owens&Minor's home office, you'll find that all offices have glass fronts that run from the ceiling to the floor. This was done on purpose as it is Gil's way of letting teammates know that Owens&Minor has an open-door policy. There's no one hiding behind walls and closed doors. It's not an uncommon occurrence to see teammates sitting in Gil's office sharing their thoughts about the company.

Teamwork

Gil understands the true meaning of teamwork and its value to the organization. He understands that every teammate brings something to the table and all are encouraged to do so. Monthly officer/teammate meetings are held where teammates meet with the officers of the company. Officers share what's taking place on their teams. Teammates are encouraged to ask questions and share information. Survey and customer service information is shared at this meeting, and those receiving OM Star Performer Awards are recognized. It's more of a celebration than a meeting, and all walk away feeling like it is time well spent.

A True Giraffe

Giraffes are able to reach things that other animals can't. Gil Minor is a true giraffe, taking his company to new and exciting heights. And, like a giraffe, it's all been accomplished without a lot of fanfare and hullabaloo. Actions speak louder than words, and Gil

Minor leads and makes the tough decisions while still exhibiting a caring and compassionate attitude. However, like the giraffe who is competitive and can kick in four directions, Gil possesses a never-say-die attitude. It is a most admirable trait and one that has propelled him, and Owens&Minor, to the top of the industry.

His name is Minor, but he makes a major difference in the lives of all those he touches. I know…he's my boss.

 Giraffism: When you stand head and shoulders above the crowd, you're looked up to by all.

EPILOGUE

I never intended to write a book. In fact as a biology/chemistry major at the Virginia Military Institute, I spelled Goldwater AuH$_2$O! That should immediately put into perspective my writing skills.

Over the years, I've given thousands of presentations and written articles for newspapers, magazines, civic organization publications, and corporate sales and marketing programs. In doing this people would suggest that I write a book and fill it full of stories about team-work, leadership, communication and customer service. They would point out that in speaking I come into contact with so many different organizations and that I needed to share those things that they were doing right and those things that could be improved upon.

One of the individuals who encouraged me to write is my friend Kevin Freiberg. He and his wife, Jackie, are co-authors of the best seller, *NUTS! Southwest Airlines' Crazy Recipe for Business and Personal Success.* I first met Kevin when I asked him to speak at the Virginia Forum for Excellence. When I met him at the convention center I sensed I was in the presence of a very special human being. His warmth, sincerity and overall demeanor were captivating and I felt like I had known him for years. We talked about life, business, family values, and what it takes to be successful. We talked about the importance of leadership, change, innovation, caring about others, unselfishness, and life-long learning. Most of all, we talked about the fact that it's important to not take yourself too seriously and to have fun at work, home and play.

Another individual who encouraged me to pen my thoughts was Jim Belasco. Jim is the author of *Teaching the Elephant to Dance, The Flight of the Buffalo, Soaring With the Phoenix,* and his most recently-released *The Ten Commandments of Success.* He is also a consultant to many businesses in the U.S. and abroad. Many of the philosophies I share in this book and in my speeches are things Jim and I have discussed. He helped me understand the value of thinking outside the box and of planning and implementing change in organizations. I figured that if he could write about dancing elephants and flying buffaloes, I could write about tall giraffes.

Throughout the book are a lot of references to positive attitudes, enthusiasm, being the best that you can be, realizing your potential, and giving. That influence is a result of the time I spent at Marble Collegiate Church in New York City listening to Norman Vincent Peale. He was a true motivator who taught me that one can overcome any of life's problems through faith in God and a belief in one's self.

They say a picture is worth a thousand words and when it comes to my co-author, Bill Gravitt, that's an understatement. Bill has the uncanny ability to create artistic work that conveys a message. His drawings are wonderful and make this book special. He has been by my side from the beginning of this process and has been so instrumental in helping me formulate my ideas.

Last but by no means least, I would not be writing this without the support of my family. My lovely wife, Nelle, who is always there for me, encouraging me all the way; my children, Cathi and Jonathan; and my step-children, Sam and Amanda. They are the loves of my life who inspire me to be the best that I can be and to make a difference in the lives of others.